M000013012

"I've just finished reading *Safe and Secure in a Tippy Canoe* and my heart is happy, my memories of my own childhood are returning, and I've got the warm-fuzzies all over. I must admit that I'm glad I didn't have to raise the author . . . he was a handful, and yet I've fallen in love with this kid. I found him endearing, and he charmed me with his adventures and his big heart. This book will fill you with a sense that at one time all was right with the world . . . CW's writing style [is] both poignant and humorous. I suggest you curl up in a comfortable chair, pull the throw over your legs, sip your favorite drink, and relive your childhood 'Spencer' style. You're in for a treat."

—Brenda Cobb Murphy, author, *The Wild Romancer*

"In a day where memoir can be dark revelations buried under the veneer of happiness and success, [this] is a refreshing feel-good look at the ups and downs of a pre-teen baby boomer growing up in a small town in Eastern Ohio . . . There's a feeling of belonging and trust, a sense of community . . . a place where neighbors watch out for neighbors, where everyone plays some part in the care and nurture of its young people. Spencer's writing style is informal, lighthearted, and fun. The reader will laugh out loud at the way the author describes adult behavior from the viewpoint of a child or frames a scene with just the right metaphor."

—Karen Power, Ph.D., Assistant Editor, the *Antioch Review*

SAFE AND SECURE IN A TIPPY CANOE

Growing up in small-town Ohio without helmets, health warnings, or helicopter parents

CW Spencer

with Bonnie Spencer

LAMP·LIGHT
PUBLISHING

ISBN-13: 978-0-9907502-1-5

Cover design by Michael L. Smith
Cover photo © 2018 Bonnie Spencer
Cover background photos are property of CW Spencer

Published by Lamp·Light Publishing

Thy word is a lamp unto my feet, and a light unto my path.
~ Psalm 119:105 (KJV)

Printed in the United States of America

To my parents,
Jim and Ann Spencer,
who let me be a kid

And to all the other "parents" I had
in Tippecanoe

CONTENTS

PREFACE

THE WAY I SEE IT, unless you had an ideal childhood, the adult years are basically a period of patch and repair. But who wants a perfect childhood? It can only be downhill from there.

Boomers love to talk about the drama they lived as kids. The breakfast crowd of 60-something men at a popular local fast-food restaurant are no exception. Though my age and early experiences qualify me to join them, I prefer my quiet table in the corner. However, I admit that I'm occasionally guilty of eavesdropping on their lively conversations.

I hear of the adventures that were an everyday part of their childhoods. They don't seem to have a problem with the dangers that went along with that free-spirited lifestyle. What they do bemoan is the shortage of risks and challenges their grandkids encounter in today's world.

They would be OK with no mandatory car seats, no required bike helmets, and fewer anti-bullying programs in the schools. Bring back a little dodgeball, allow a swat here and there, and let kids fight it out once in a while. Oh yeah, and dole out a few less trophies, maybe just to those who earn them. Kind of like the real world they will one day find themselves in.

Some young people may raise their eyebrows when they hear those guys. Who are those Neanderthals? But I understand them. I, too, lean toward old-school child-rearing. Less coddling, more independence. That's how it was for me when I lived in Tippecanoe, a small town in eastern Ohio in the early 1960s. Those were the genuine good old days: minimal restrictions on my time and activities, license to roam the countryside, freedom to be a kid.

It's probably my duty as an old codger to do a little bemoaning myself on how childhood has changed. But I'll try to resist. Instead, I'll share how I was raised and let you draw your own conclusions. Despite the glaring lack of safety precautions, I was a happy and secure child. I wouldn't have wanted to spend those years in any other way—or in any other place.

Tippecanoe held a certain storybook charm, and it was the source of some of my most cherished memories. A drink of Johnny Appleseed's icy spring water in the dog days of August. My first and totally unwanted taste of pizza. The "catch" that made me a hometown celebrity. An unexpected friendship with the reclusive Cookie Lady. The pride in my dad's eyes, despite a royal mess-up on my part. This was my beloved Tippecanoe.

The people in this book are real except for a minor character or two who are composites of people I have known. To respect everyone's privacy, I have changed their names. All but those of my family who, no doubt, will wish they were not exceptions.

Most of the incidents in these pages really did happen. However, due to some stubbornly stuck drawers in the deep-storage filing cabinets of my brain, I built some chapters upon mere memory fragments. Where my recollections are fuzzy, I have taken the liberty to add details that would be compatible with the reality of that time and the individuals involved.

And one last caveat. This is my life as I remember it half a century later. My perceptions may not be the same as someone else's. To those of you who may recognize yourselves in these pages and view the events through a different lens, I hope you will enjoy this story for what it is: a nostalgic look at growing up in small-town Ohio in the 1960s—through the eyes of a day-dreamy little kid.

Prologue

My Starting Point

I WAS THRUST INTO THE WORLD sporting a pronounced cone-shaped head. My parents' word is all I have on that, though, since it appears no one had the courage to take a picture. I am left with a mental image of my triangular baby head displaying a mouth eight inches wide and eyeballs nearly touching. African Mangbetu women would have been overjoyed to have such a head start with their newborns.

In the nineteenth century, the Mangbetu tribe in northeastern Congo practiced Lipombo, the art of head elongation. While a baby's skull was still soft, the mother wrapped it tightly with cloth or cord. As the head grew, she replaced the wrappings until she achieved the shape she wanted. The lengthened head signified status among the ruling class. It also indicated intelligence because they believed they were increasing the size of the brain cavity.

By the time my already-elongated head arrived on the scene, Lipombo was dying out. So had my parents even known about this regal practice, it was no longer fashionable. But they didn't know. And being first-time parents, it crushed them. Dad wanted a son to follow him into the lumber business. He realized, though, that it would be next to impossible to find a hardhat to fit me.

I can imagine Dad, in spite of his disappointment, trying to cheer Mom up in the hospital. "It won't be so bad, Anna. The boy could dye his hair orange and be a highway worker with a built-in traffic cone. Or he could stand outside public restrooms to warn people of freshly mopped floors. He'd even be able to move himself—a cone with a brain. Our son will never be out of work."

I can also imagine Mom, after three days of hard labor, looking around for a bedpan to flatten Dad's head.

Fortunately for both Dad and me, *my* head would be the one reshaped. Discovering my skull to be pliable, Dad and Mom did their own cranial modification. For the next few days, they took turns at sculpting my head into something a little more sphere-ish.

Since the reverse Lipombo likely downsized my brain cavity, I don't know what effect it had on my IQ. Dad's long-range plans for me looked brighter, though. My head wasn't round, but at least they had modified the point enough to reduce any future hardhat wobble. And my parents had gained invaluable experience in case their next child took after me in the head department.

Paula joined our family next, then Lloyd, both with nearly normal noggins. Dad must have been very grateful to God; a few years later he became a born-again Christian. He lost interest in the sawmill (all that head shaping for nothing) and looked for a temporary factory job in the city. He found work that allowed him to study at night for his ordination into the Methodist Church.

Meanwhile, I was becoming more and more the outdoor type, largely because Dad and Mom seemed reluctant to let me in the house. I galloped around on our five acres pretending to be my hero, the Lone Ranger. My broomstick horse Silver could easily rear up on his one wooden leg to imitate his namesake.

Though I didn't completely abandon the masked man, when I was seven Tom Terrific debuted on *Captain Kangaroo* and instantly became my new hero. I routinely wore my funnel thinking cap and yelled to no one in particular that I was Tom Terrific. I sang his theme song all day long while changing myself into whatever the situation called for. Tom was a treasure chest for my young imagination. And let's face it—my head was *born* for the character.

Just as Mom found out she was pregnant again, Dad completed his ordination and received his assignment to three tiny churches in eastern Ohio. The family packed for our 150-mile move south to Tippecanoe. Dad was torn as to whether the funnel should make the move. By that time I had outgrown my pointy head, but now he was eager for me to outgrow Tom Terrific. Minutes before the moving van pulled away, Dad tossed the metal hat into the box with my black mask. Maybe God meant for me to sport a cone—and it wouldn't be wise for a new minister to sabotage God's plans.

Chapter 1

Sugar Highs and Lows

I TRIED HARD to think of something I hated worse than family meetings. A heaping tablespoon of extra-gooey castor oil? Possibly a drilling session in the dentist's chair? Maybe Mercurochrome splashed on a raw, open laceration? Any one of these tortures would have been preferable to the meeting taking place in the Spencer home that Saturday morning.

To help cope, I daydreamed of the events that had taken place earlier in the week. It had been one of my best weeks ever. We had moved just the week before, but I had already found Tippecanoe and the surrounding countryside to be a magical place. Stillwater Creek with its dark mysteries flowed around the west side of town. On the other side was cold, deep Clendening Lake, separated from the parsonage by only a few hills. Those Appalachian Foothills seemed like mountains to our family. The memory of the flat snowbelt of northern Ohio was already melting away.

When I wasn't pedaling my bike over the sidewalks, streets,

and alleys of our new community, Dad was driving the family around in his two-tone '58 Ford. The distinctively different landscape of Tippecanoe enthralled everyone, but no one more so than me. It was during one of those rides that my ten-year-old still-forming brain perceived a calling from above. As far as I could tell, I had been divinely handpicked to explore this new land, to pave the way for other ten-year-olds who wanted a fresh start.

I had drunk to that mission, though secretly, the night before at the A&W Root Beer stand located a few miles south of town. The entire family had drunk to Dad's new churches and a new beginning for all of us. As the foam tickled my nose, I wondered how things could get any better.

They wouldn't, at least not that next morning due to the untimely family meeting. In 25 minutes the Lone Ranger would make his weekly TV appearance. Though the show took valuable Saturday outdoor time, somebody had to help Tonto cover Kemo Sabe's back. My favorite duo counted on me to be there on the other side of the screen every week. (Like I said, my brain was still developing.) But entertainment had ceased while three other captives and I waited to see what would come down.

Paula, a year and a half younger than me and eager to please, tried to look interested in family business. My brother Lloyd sat relaxed and unconcerned. At six years old, he was satisfied to go with the flow. Mom probably wanted the meeting to end more than any of us so she could visit her new friend Marge.

We soon discovered that Dad had called the meeting to get the family in line. First on the agenda was the previous night's frothy celebration. There were to be limits on refills in the future. That might not be so bad. Temperance sounded pretty good at the moment, considering the stomach pains I had suffered during the night. That morning I had even cut down the sugar on my Wheaties to two tablespoons. I hoped this was all Dad had, but I had a sneaky feeling it wasn't.

As I suspected, item one had only been the head of bubbles. Dad's underlying reason for summoning us was that he wanted to make a good impression in his new churches. Tomorrow he would present the entire family to all three congregations, starting in West Chester, then going on to Stillwater, and ending up in his main church in Tippecanoe, which sat next door to the parsonage.

Dad quickly got down to business and told us all to "listen good." Besides the other distractions, my head still ached from my root beer hangover, so it was through a hazy sarsaparilla fog I heard him reel off three new directives: there would be no more running all over the place, there would be no more acting stupid, and there would be no more hooliganism.

I felt myself start to slip into shock. Besides eating and sleeping, this was who I was. Well, I wasn't exactly sure what hooliganism was, but it sounded to me like something that could be found in my portfolio.

Dad further rattled me when he added, "Do you understand, Clarence?" First of all, there were others at the meeting who needed to understand it too. Second, I didn't like to be reminded of my real name.

When I was in good standing, I was Butch, and I liked being Butch. I complained once when Dad called me Clarence. His response was, "Your grandfather's name is Clarence. Don't you like him?" I wasn't articulate enough at the time to counter with,

"Yes, I *love* Grandpa; I just don't like his *name*." If there was a connection, it wasn't clear to me.

Neither were the new rules clear to me. What did Dad mean by "acting stupid"? He needed to spell out some stupid specifics. Did he mean things like going outside with no coat in 30-degree weather, sticking noodles up my nose, or digging pointless holes all over the backyard? And what would be my defense if he accused me of "running all over the place"? The lack of clarity meant I had little hope of an acquittal. I felt panicky. My exciting and adventurous life in this new territory was about to end almost before it got started.

My first hope was that Lloyd would voice some objections. However, Dad and Mom would likely just smile and coo: *how cute; he will go far, that boy; he sure knows how to speak his mind.*

So I considered the unthinkable. I would tell Dad I hated him and stomp out, slamming the door to add an exclamation point. I might actually survive since it would look bad for the first funeral he officiated in Tippecanoe to be for his oldest child following a family squabble. On the other hand, it would send a powerful message to his new congregation regarding sin and its consequences.

I realized my only *real* hope was that Dad would be too busy with his three new churches to follow up on his new regulations.

~ ~ ~

THE MEETING ENDED in time for me to catch the last half of the show. After the Lone Ranger and Tonto rode off over the horizon, I went outside and started bouncing a rubber ball against the church foundation. I hoped that wasn't breaking any of the new rules. Jerry and Eddie, two boys my age I had met earlier in the week, showed up to play. Their game that day was to keep the ball away from the new kid.

It was fun for about 30 seconds; then I started to get upset. I was no match against the pair. I could see that being the preacher's kid carried little weight with them. It was decision time. Would I be Tom Terrific or the Lone Ranger? Either hero was capable of getting my ball back.

Even though Mom had not unpacked my funnel yet, I decided on Tom. I could become a giant catcher's mitt and snag my ball on a toss. A bowling ball could knock the guys over; then a quick switch to a German shepherd and I could scoop up the dropped ball. Or I could change into a bumblebee and sting them till they gave up. One of these expressions of Tom's superpowers should be able to get the job done.

After two minutes of morphing, Tom was no more successful than I had been. I gave up and quit playing their game. Immediately they returned my ball. Who knew that was all I needed to do?

All was forgiven when Eddie and Jerry announced they were going to take me to see the Cookie Lady. They said she always had a fresh batch of baked goodies waiting after lunch. It was early afternoon, so I'd finally metabolized the overdose of sugar from the evening before. And I was never one to turn down any sweets.

The amount of sugar we consumed never seemed to overly concern Dad and Mom. Every so often, though, they tried to discourage our intake a bit by telling us that all our teeth would fall out if we ate too much. I always wondered if that could really happen. Even so, it didn't diminish our sugar cravings, and they let us eat our sweets. But we also had sure better eat the healthy fare put in front of us come mealtime.

I decided to not ask permission to go with Eddie and Jerry and just hope no one would notice I was gone. This action potentially broke two of the three new rules. Maybe all of them, but I still didn't know what hooliganism entailed.

The three of us followed the gravel alley beside the church as it inclined gradually to the edge of the woods. Then we turned onto a lane that veered left through the trees and ascended sharply. Although we were not far behind the parsonage, I hadn't discovered this territory yet.

Five minutes later, near the top of the hill, we reached our destination. When I saw the creepy joker-like gargoyles perched atop two stone gateposts, I thought for the first time that obeying the new family rules might be a good idea. As we passed between the guards, I stayed so close to Eddie and Jerry that I practically tripped over them. I hoped my new friends knew what they were doing.

Three cats scattered from the path, a black one hissing in our direction as it disappeared into a patch of tall grass and thistles. A thick ring of towering, gnarly trees edged the property. I was sure that after dark there would be pairs of glowing eyeballs staring out from them, assisting the gargoyles in their duties.

The phrase "cookie lady" had created in my mind a vision of a multicolored cottage with flashing neon lights, but the house that loomed before us was dark and drab. At one time it might have been brightly adorned, but now it didn't wear a lick of paint. The door sounded thick as Eddie used the knocker that bore the head of a hungry-looking canine.

When the door creaked open, a blast of sweet peanut butter cookie dough fragrance hit me in the face. In the doorway stood an ancient lady in a long white dress. Her kind, inviting smile, along with my olfactory findings, caused my apprehension to drift away. She led us to a couch before disappearing in the direction of the source of the intoxicating aroma.

The room was dark, but as my eyes adjusted, I was able to see it was full of fancy old-fashioned furniture. Several more cats lounged on the velvet couch and chairs or roamed around the clean, uncluttered room. The carpet, somewhat faded and worn, bore designs of castles and knights with swords. A chandelier hung in the middle of the high ceiling. The crystals caught the one bright sunray that found its way through an opening in the heavy drapes and broke the light into rainbow colors that danced around the room. This was not your average cookie joint.

Nor were the cookies the lady returned with average in any way. They required both hands. When I took my first bite, I felt as though I'd walked through the gates of cookie heaven. As she stood smiling at three grateful kids with cookie crumbs and milk rings around their mouths, I could have sworn she was wearing a pair of wings.

~ ~ ~

WE HAD SUPPER EARLY ON SATURDAY so Dad could get plenty of sleep for his big day Sunday. I stared at the heaping plate of liver and broccoli that sat in front of me. Then I recalled the three saucer-sized peanut butter masterpieces I had eaten just a couple of hours before. I had no room to stuff in any more food, at least not what was on that night's menu. Some foods take up more room in the stomach than others—and broccoli and liver are near the top of that list.

It wouldn't work to knock my plate off the table. That would earn me a scolding and a clean plate piled even higher. An "accidental" self-inflicted stab with my fork would only lead to a Mercurochrome sloshing. An imaginary toothache? Unfortunately, that would get me a *real* trip to the dentist. My options were nonexistent, so I forced the food down in microbites. Maybe everyone else would finish the meal way before me and I could kindly offer to clear the dishes.

As I choked down another sliver of liver, Dad began talking about his visitation list. It included several people who didn't attend church. One name caught my attention: Trulah Gilbody. He said she was an elderly lady who lived in a run-down house at the top of the hill behind the parsonage. *Run-down house? Behind the parsonage?* He had heard gargoyles guarded the gate. *Gargoyles?* Dad said emphatically that was one place none of us were to go, at least not until he had a chance to visit first and check it out. *Too late,* my mind sang.

I took bigger bites and cleaned my plate, silently swearing off sugary treats forever.

~ ~ ~

IT WAS CERTAINLY NOT DAD'S HABIT to share gossip with his family, but the next day he told us what he had heard about the gargoyle house, no doubt to keep us kids from venturing up there. For years, every weekend like clockwork, townspeople observed a lady driving an aged Packard up the alley toward Trulah Gilbody's place. They speculated as to what the two ladies were up to, especially since they never attended Sunday services. There were rumors they might be moonshiners, or that Mrs. Gilbody might even be a witch.

Dad felt duty-bound to check out the situation. He wasn't in a hurry though. Multiple sources had warned him she might eat him alive. Mrs. Gilbody's name kept getting moved further down the visitation list. Not that Dad was a coward. Cowards didn't volunteer to be Rangers in the war. Let's just say he was prudently cautious.

~ ~ ~

TWO WEEKS LATER Dad finally laid aside some of his caution and warily ascended the hill to make the visit.

At supper that night, he announced, "I met Trulah Gilbody today."

My green beans nearly came back up. What if my trip there— no, multiply that by four—had been found out? At the thought of a castor oil remedy, I commanded the beans to stay put.

Dad continued. "We had a long chat. She's a very nice lady. Her husband died about ten years ago in a car accident. She talked about her sister, Genevieve, who is coming tomorrow to bring her groceries and supplies."

"That's who comes to see her every week?" Mom asked.

"Yes. They have church together on Sunday mornings, just as the Gilbody family has done for generations up on that hill. We read the Bible together while I was there."

"Maybe she'll come to our services," Mom said. "I can go see her next week. I'll take her a coffee cake and ask her to church."

"Already done. I invited her to come down, and bring her sister, but she politely declined. She did say maybe someday. But she's more interested in some of the church members coming *up* the hill and getting to know her instead of making up rumors."

"I wonder how she hears the rumors," Mom said.

"Kids go snooping around her place to satisfy their curiosity.

Sometimes they get a little loud. She says she has excellent hearing."

I slid down in my seat and scrutinized my chicken leg.

Mom said, "That must make her feel like no one cares about her. I'll still pay her a visit soon."

"She told me she actually gets a kick out of some of the things she hears. I got the impression she might have even started one or two of them herself," he chuckled.

I peered over my chicken. At that moment, I knew that Trulah Gilbody and my dad were kindred spirits. They both liked to stir the pot once in a while.

Dad's relationship with the Cookie Lady could be a good thing, I thought.

However, I still wondered if she had told Dad about the many visits I had already made to the forbidden house.

"By the way," Dad said, "Miss Gilbody offered to make peanut butter cookies for me to take to our next church pot-luck supper." Then he looked straight at me. "I've heard they're the best *some* people around here have ever tasted."

Dad winked at me, and for the time being, all was well with the world. Even if all my teeth fell out that very second.

Chapter 2

Sharp Pointy Things

THE SPENCER FAMILY took a trip to Dr. Trimnell's that first summer. Or maybe I should say we went on an expedition. His house was located outside of town. His driveway turned off the main road and went forever. It was edged with trees that canopied to form a curious dark tunnel. I imagined we were deep in the jungle. I peered out the window hoping to catch a glimpse of monkeys swinging over our car.

We finally reached the steep-roofed stone house. It was much larger than the houses in town. My parents led the way into Dr. Trimnell's den that doubled as his waiting room. Just inside the musty room, a monstrous stuffed lion greeted us. The heads of boars, rhinos, and other hapless victims populated the walls. We kids sat down in the permanently crowded room and nervously awaited our turns.

Dr. Trimnell was mysterious, but not unfriendly. He puffed on a long, curved pipe with a huge bowl. After some friendly chit-chat among the adults, Dad told him to catch us up on our shots for school. Being the oldest, I was the first one taken into the examination room.

The strong disinfectant smell almost overpowered me as it merged with the syrupy sweet odor of Dr. Trimnell's tobacco. But I immediately snapped out of it when I saw the array of needles on the counter. Judging by their size, they must have been used in his big game tranquilizer gun. I feared I might become his next trophy. He called me a big man. He must have been trying to justify the big needles. Though I appreciated his unrealistic reference to my stature and place in the community, I decided to stay healthy and avoid any more visits until I really *was* a big man.

I was still feeling the effects of Dr. Trimnell's needles the following day. It was hard to sit on my bike seat. I was willing to endure the discomfort, however, since bike riding was becoming my main summer pastime.

Our parents placed few restrictions on my friends and me. We could ride our bikes all day from one end of town to the other, and even beyond. Neither we nor our parents feared any harm would come to us. I just needed to tell Mom I was leaving on my bike and she would say to be back by mealtime. No one required us to wear bike helmets either. That was good, for all I had was the funnel. And I wasn't even sure where that was. I hadn't had much to do with Tom Terrific since the not-so-terrific keep-away game.

I had made another friend in my grade. Bruce was about a head taller than me and played center on the basketball team. His parents owned one of the two grocery stores in town. The family lived upstairs. This made it convenient for Bruce and his younger siblings to pilfer from the candy jars. Whenever Paula, Lloyd, or I stayed at their house all night, we got to share in the spoils. It's no surprise that Bruce's house became our favorite overnight spot.

Bruce lived on the other side of SR 8, the road that ran in front of the parsonage and the church. It was far from being a superhighway, but it was the main thoroughfare through town and Dad didn't trust me on it. He took me out there for a talking to. I was to be extra careful on that road. I was to use my head and be responsible. Just because I was a preacher's kid didn't mean I had special protection. He didn't need to tell me that. I had already discovered that being a PK wasn't a privileged position. In fact, I figured there might be a motorist or two who might even speed up to take me out and get some brownie points with the devil.

Not even a week had passed before I was almost hit crossing the road on my bike to see Bruce. Dad was on the porch and saw it all. I got a talking to that far exceeded the previous one. It was worse than getting hit would have been. He showed me the skid marks close up and said I was lucky the driver was able to stop. The marks stayed there for weeks, a reminder to the entire town that I was living on borrowed time.

Even worse, I now had to get Mom or Dad to escort me across the road whether I was walking or riding. Besides it being the ultimate embarrassment, it always came with another skid-mark lecture. Fortunately, Jerry and Eddie lived on my side of the road, and we had plenty there to occupy us. I probably could have gone all summer without crossing the road. But one thing made the lecture—and humiliation—tolerable every few days. That was a visit to Johnny's place.

~ ~ ~

WE NEVER KNEW HIS REAL NAME, but all the kids called him Johnny Appleseed. He lived on the west side of town, just over Stillwater Creek. His log cabin sat by the road, at the bottom of a large wooded hill. He had no yard to speak of. Just north of his rustic abode, water from an icy cold spring emerged from an iron pipe and collected in a half oak barrel. Every time Bruce and I visited, we would find big bright red apples floating in the barrel. Sometimes they were still bobbing.

We'd each grab an apple and fill our canteens with the tasty spring water before heading up to the house. We could usually find Johnny sitting on his porch, which extended across the front of the cabin and was edged with his menagerie of animal wood carvings. Johnny also carved faces on the tops of walking sticks and even into his furniture. My favorite was Bigfoot. It wouldn't have surprised me one bit if the huge hairy creature had sat in one of Johnny's log chairs and posed while the two of them grunted at each other.

Johnny was the second "misfit" adult I met that summer. Like the Cookie Lady, he had little association with the people in town. But since Dad had sampled Johnny's spring water and porch more than once, he had no qualms about me hanging out there.

The large bearded man of few words knew his stuff. The first time I visited Johnny, I watched in awe as he transformed a piece of wood into a small bear. When he finished, he took an apple from a box beside his chair and said, "Like this." He started from the top and peeled the apple all in one long spiral ribbon. He motioned for my knife, gave it just a lick or two with his whetstone, and then showed me how to hold it for my first try on my own apple. Before I left that day, he looked me in the eyes and said, "You are a big man with a sharp knife, so no more mumbley peg, you hear?" For a recluse, he seemed to know what went on in town.

All the boys played mumbley peg. One version was to stick your pocketknife in the ground by way of a series of tricky throws. We usually played the shortcut version though: just see who could make it stick closest to his own foot. The winner pounded a stick into the ground—that was the mumbley peg—and the loser had to pull it out with his teeth. If excess sugar didn't destroy our teeth, a mumbley peg could well do the job. My teeth were probably not Johnny's concern though.

It took two weeks of watching Johnny and practicing for me to peel my apple all in one piece. Then he moved on to lessons on carving animals. By then he had a pretty good edge on my blade. Every time he sharpened my blade a little more he asked, "You playin' mumbley peg?" I gave him a truthful no. So did Bruce. Something about Johnny commanded respect. We didn't ever want to disappoint him. Besides, my knife was sharp enough by then to take off a toe or two.

But while I became more responsible and skilled with my prized jackknife, I ushered in a new meaning to the word stupid in another arena.

~ ~ ~

I WAS EIGHT when my grandfather introduced me to his carbide lamp. He would load it up, add the water, and light it. Then he would hand it to me, and we would walk around his large pond at night. Grandpa liked to make me feel big, and he knew just how to do it.

I couldn't see what was happening inside the lamp, so Grandpa showed me the explosive reaction of dropping a pellet of calcium carbide into water. That might have been the event that began my path toward becoming a science teacher. For sure, it lit a desire for some of those fizzy rocks for my own experimentation. But the craving cooled to embers over the next couple of years.

The flame was reignited one day when I was in the hardware store and saw a blue can just like Grandpa's. I waited till Dad was in a really good mood and asked him for some calcium carbide. The question was enough to change his mood, and I knew I would be old and gray before he would allow me to have any.

I didn't have to wait that long though. It turned out Bruce had some in his garage. Being the obedient child I was, I had Mom walk me across SR 8 so I could go play with carbide.

I found Bruce in his garage. He usually had more sense than I did so he wasn't totally onboard with the idea at first. When I spotted the forbidden blue can sitting on the workbench, a shiver of excitement rushed through me. Before long my enthusiasm for flammable and explosive gas won Bruce over. We rummaged in the trash can for suitable containers for our experiment.

Bruce found an open metal soup can. I chose a thick glass ketchup bottle. I thought my container was way superior because I would be able to see the reaction better. We both poured water into our containers. Then Bruce dropped a couple pellets into his can. We watched intently as the rocks danced around in the bubbly mixture. After two minutes, it fizzled out.

It was my turn. With trembling hands I loaded a half dozen of the pellets into my bottle. The bubbling was immediate. When I screwed on the cap, the fizzing stopped. Realizing the bottle needed a way to release the gas, I quickly removed the cap, pounded a hole in it, and screwed it back on.

Bruce had matches. My parents didn't allow me to light matches, but I hoped that in this case two wrongs might somehow make a right. When they saw my ingenuity and realized how clever I was, they would be so proud of their son.

We stepped outside the garage. I lit the gas coming from my bottle, and a perfect flame appeared. Life was good. I was beaming with pride. I had made my own torch.

With such a wonderful accomplishment under my belt, I wanted to do something productive with it. I decided to do some welding on Bruce's swing set in the middle of the yard. However, I didn't even make it ten feet.

The bottle exploded violently in my hand and covered me with the hot, smelly liquid. Bruce freaked out and suddenly decided he heard his mom calling him in. Alone in his yard, I tasted blood. I felt a huge gash in my nose right between my eyes where a shard of glass had struck me. The panic of nearly losing an eye, however, paled to what I felt when I thought of having to go home and confess.

~ ~ ~

I HADN'T PLANNED TO LIE, but when I walked in and saw Mom first, I figured maybe I had a chance to get away with this one. I told her I had been playing at Bruce's and had fallen on a sharp edge of the swing set. When she saw all the blood, she ran and got Dad and told him my story.

They wiped off the blood and the spent carbide (that I had never used) and whisked me off to Dr. Trimnell's. It had only been a month since I had gotten acquainted with his needles. When I had pledged to stay healthy, I hadn't accounted for the visits due to injuries.

Dr. Trimnell and my Dad discussed my situation. I didn't hear much of it through my blubbering. I caught enough though. They decided that nothing would be used to numb the cleaning and stitching, being that the injury was so close to my eyes. Getting those stitches was worse than castor oil, Mercurochrome, and a dentist visit combined.

I must have been reeking of carbide, and Dad wasn't stupid. But he never confronted me about my concocted story. He, like the other adults in town, was not afraid to let his kids do a little reaping of what they sowed. And Dad knew that sometimes he needed to step aside and trust God to work in his wayward son.

It was evident that I would not become a "big man" automatically. Those growing pains could be downright excruciating, especially when they hit you right between the eyes.

Chapter 3

Imposed Values

PARENTS TODAY are expected to explain their reasoning on every single do and don't. When I was growing up, there must not have been any "explanation" clause in their job description. If kids had the nerve to question a policy, the answer we nearly always got was, "Because I'm your dad (or mom) and I said so." I soon learned not to ask.

Take the matter of church attendance. I thought kids should be able to decide for themselves whether to go. OK, maybe make it compulsory for Christmas and Easter. Those were the two times we got candy rewards for going. But the Spencer kids did not get a vote; our parents required us to attend without any discussion. (I was more lenient with my own offspring. I allowed them discourse on the topic, then gave them options: church and lunch, or no church and no lunch. They never went hungry.)

If given a choice, I would have stayed home from church once or twice to see what it was like. I wondered what might be on

Sunday morning TV. Probably not much for kids since they all had to be in church. If I had been free to run around outside during the service, I would have been running by myself. That wouldn't have been so much fun. Still, a kid likes to find these things out for himself.

Sunday school was different. That was because Hopalong Cassidy talked to us kids about it after his show one day. It went something like this: "Someone told me that some of you kids out there have been giving your moms trouble about going to Sunday school." I dropped my head in shame. He was talking about me in front of millions of viewers. "Do Hoppy a favor and smile when she takes you. Hoppy goes, you know." That was all I needed to hear. Hoppy's values were my values, and there was never another problem for Mom on that account.

~ ~ ~

MORE RULES BEGAN TRICKLING DOWN from the top. No playing with carbide (after the fact); no going to Clendening Lake (I'd already been there but they didn't know . . . I didn't think); and no talking and giggling during church services. Although the newest rules were more specific than the Big Three, I found that clarity didn't make them easier to follow, after all.

It wasn't that I was a bad kid, just that curiosity oozed from my pores. Also, the fact that something was banned jumped around in my mind like popcorn in a heated Jiffy Pop pan and, inevitably, led me to do that very thing.

For a while, I did pretty well with the ban on talking and giggling in church. No doubt that was due to the fact that my family sat in the front row and my dad could hear all and see all from behind the raised pulpit. Tippecanoe Methodist Church was tiny.

Real tiny. Dad could just about reach out and grab me from where he stood.

Location aside, you'd think it would be easy not to laugh during the serious segments of the message. The wages of sin are not funny. However, solemn situations often spawned an uncontrollable urge to laugh. Each Sunday I tried to vent my laughter during the sanctioned times when Dad told jokes. If I'd heard them already, or even if I didn't get them, I laughed enthusiastically. I just had to be careful not to be the last one laughing.

This worked well for me until one unfortunate Sunday. I should have been smart enough not to look over at Jerry sitting in the front pew across the aisle. He was always making goofy faces at me.

Dad never picked up on Jerry's front-row shenanigans. He was too focused on his number one son. Besides, he expected nothing less than exemplary behavior from Jerry. My parents admired him. He used the appropriate words when talking to adults: please, thank you, sir, and ma'am. He could play grownups like violins. His alter ego set the bar pretty much beyond my reach.

This particular Sunday as Dad was delving into his third point, my eyes snapped to Jerry like iron to a magnet. He crossed his eyes at me and pulled his ears out as far as he could. A huge knot of undetermined emotion twisted in pain deep inside of me. If I allowed it to escape the bonds of my four-and-a-half-foot frame, I suspected it might burst forth as joy. But it was not the time or place for joy. This was adult church.

No jokes were forthcoming in the sermon. I squirmed. I coughed. I bit my cheeks, counted backwards, and held my breath. I tried to think dark, scary thoughts to suppress a giggle or worse. Nothing worked.

I sure could be a dummy sometimes. I took one more high-risk look at Jerry. Mom must have been looking at him, too, because he was sitting there like the angel she thought he was. Jerry's radar could always detect an adult's glance in his direction.

The sight of Jerry wearing his pretend halo was too much for me. The knot unraveled, and I erupted during the most solemn part of the sermon. It was no small exhibition. People in the street could have heard me. No one in the congregation knew what to do. They didn't dare crack a smile knowing how much trouble I was in. It might get them into hot water with the preacher, too.

Of course Jerry smiled, but only when his radar gave the all-clear. When Mom glanced his way again, he expressed his fake annoyance at my behavior. Mom nodded back her agreement.

~ ~ ~

ROASTED CLARENCE was on the lunch menu in the parsonage that day. Dad addressed me by my given name. I guess *Butch* didn't have a stern enough ring to it.

He questioned me. "What was so funny in church today, Clarence? Can you see I'm not laughing? Do you see anyone else here laughing?"

Even under this intense interrogation, I felt a snicker rising up. Everyone else around the table looked as though they were working hard to stifle giggles too. I wanted to transport myself to Jerry's lunch table where I would be free to laugh as much as I wanted.

~ ~ ~

THE FOLLOWING WEEK was a downer. Dad never mentioned any punishment, but I had a strong feeling he wasn't happy with me. I dreaded Sunday, afraid he would unleash his wrath on me in front of his flock.

My day of reckoning arrived. Dad took his place behind the pulpit and surveyed the congregation. No jokes appeared to be forthcoming. *So much for my laughter-venting time.* Then he said something that seemed to have nothing to do with his sermon, taking everyone by surprise.

"I guess I should say something about my oldest son Clarence's behavior last week." Everyone looked at each other wondering if the preacher had another son he hadn't introduced yet—and probably questioning who would give a name like that to their kid. Following Dad's gaze, the congregation collectively realized that *Butch* wasn't my given name.

Despite my anxiety over what Dad was about to say, another forbidden laugh was building. This could literally be my *last* laugh, I thought.

"I have been thinking a lot about his outburst last week," Dad continued. "And I've done some soul searching. I asked myself, 'Don't you suppose Jesus laughed a time or two?'" He let that sink in for a few moments.

"Sometimes a laugh is just good for the soul, don't you agree?" The little church could hardly contain all the smiles in response. Then he looked at me with a grin in his eyes. "But my son will try to restrain himself just a bit today, won't he?" The sight of me nodding vigorously made everyone laugh, long and hard.

The issue was settled. I had received grace, and the congregation saw Dad bestow it. A contented grin from ear to ear replaced my urge for another laughing fit. I was so confident that I looked over at Jerry. I could tell from his envious expression that, at that moment, he wished *he* were the preacher's son.

~ ~ ~

MY FORCED INTERNMENT IN CHURCH accomplished my father's purpose: a few years later, I became a follower of Christ. Even though my shortcomings would continue to surface and prove my humanity, alongside them was always grace bestowing blessings on me that I didn't deserve.

One day Dad told me he was proud of me. I asked him how that could be with all my bad behavior. He looked at me with forced sternness and said, "Because I'm your father and I said so." There was no further explanation or discussion—but it was all the answer I needed.

Chapter 4

Religion in School

SUMMER VACATION always started on Memorial Day. No assigned summer reading lists or family educational projects invaded that sacred time. For three months, kids censored the word *school* among themselves. Even parents tried to respect the ban.

It was no different in my new community. However, all too soon Labor Day was upon us. At the church picnic at Clendening Dam, I was praying for the impossible—that summer vacation would never end. My parents also prayed, but theirs was a prayer of thanks.

Regardless of any prayers, Tuesday morning saw a hundred or so kids and four educators make their way to the north end of town to begin or resume their journeys down the hallowed halls of learning.

Tippecanoe School had eight grades divided among the four teachers. I was in fifth grade. With Paula in third and Lloyd in first, the Spencer family had three of the four classrooms covered. Since the fourth sibling was not even on the scene yet, we would never be able to make a full sweep of the school.

Mrs. Martin began the morning by taking attendance as she seated us. She arranged her fifth graders alphabetically in the first two rows, then the sixth graders in the other two. As she welcomed us back and talked about the exciting things the year held for us, we cringed every time we heard the *S* word. Apparently she noticed because she told us to give it a day and we would be back in the routine. It wasn't that school was so awful. It was just that the abrupt transition from unbridled vacation to classroom confinement was a shock to our psyches.

Next she directed us to a poster on the wall. Under the title of "Golden Rule" was a Bible verse in fancy writing. *Therefore all things whatsoever ye would that men should do to you, do ye even so to them.* My brain was relieved when she translated it for us: Treat others like you want to be treated. These words I could understand without having to think so hard. The preliminaries ended with the pledge and a prayer.

When Mrs. Martin asked for volunteers to help pass out books, every hand went up. Besides being eager to please our teacher, we all wanted a chance to be mobile again after sitting an entire twenty minutes. She assigned the upperclassmen a chapter to read from their history books, then lectured to my half of the room.

After half an hour, she gave us some follow-up questions and switched her attention back to the other side. Mrs. Martin's smile and enthusiasm were contagious, and she planted a seed of hope in me that shifting gears to learning mode wouldn't be so bad.

From day one, I worked as fast as I could because what I got done in class would not rob me of precious bike riding time after school. But a more immediate drive was the chance to escape the confines of the classroom for a few minutes. The first student to finish his work got to choose a partner to take the dirty erasers to the creek and pound out the dust on the rocks. We usually ended up pounding them on each other. Then we looked under stones for crawdads or shot creek water at each other from smuggled squirt guns. Who could blame us for trying to hang on to some of that summer freedom?

Mrs. Martin was fair and compassionate. She didn't allow the consistent winners of speedy classwork to keep picking the same classmates. And she expected us to occasionally pick kids who never finished first so everyone would get a turn. She was always working on our character so that we might voluntarily share our good fortune. It worked. We often chose well without being forced. It was that Golden Rule thing.

Everyone in Mrs. Martin's class worked hard as far as I remember. None of us wanted to disappoint her. We admired and respected our teachers, but no one more than Mrs. Martin. She rarely raised her voice. She didn't need to because she had The Look mastered. It was an expression of disapproval that shamed us out of further mischief for a very long time.

During the periods when I had my work done and I wasn't doing dust duty, I listened to the sixth-grade lessons. I wasn't focused as much on learning, though, as I was on a particular sixth-grade girl. It was as close as I could get to a romance with Sarah Parker.

~ ~ ~

I'D HAD A SECRET CRUSH ON SARAH from the day I met her that first summer in Tippecanoe. But every time I got within fifty feet of her, I became tongue-tied and stupid. I had a little more control of my faculties in class. Even though Sarah sat only two rows away, I could speak almost coherently when Mrs. Martin asked me questions. It was as if an invisible wall separated the two grades. I never figured out how Mrs. Martin pulled that off.

At the end of each day, the upperclassmen got to leave the room first. They had to pass through that wall and traverse fifth-grade territory on their way to the coat racks and the door. Sarah would walk close to my desk. One day I shocked myself when I handed her a note at dismissal time. I didn't see her reaction because that would have involved eye contact.

I was proud of what I had penned to her. *I like you. I know you hate me. Butch.* If that didn't get the girl, I didn't know what more I could do.

The next morning, a neatly folded sheet of notebook paper appeared on my desk as Sarah passed by. My heart raced. What would I do if she liked me too? The seriousness of the situation hit me. Lucky for me that students could bow their heads to pray in school without being frowned upon.

After *Amen*, I made sure Mrs. Martin wasn't looking. With shaky hands I unfolded the paper. Sarah had written her words precisely. Her message, however, was not so precise. *I don't hate you Butch. I don't hate anybody. Sarah.*

What was that supposed to mean? I didn't know what I was hoping for, but I knew that wasn't it. Oh well, maybe I'd try again in a month or two. I decided it was time to focus more on academics, crawdads, and squirt guns. And that wouldn't leave me much time for a steady girlfriend.

~ ~ ~

OCCASIONALLY, MY CLASSMATES would call me the teacher's pet. The kids stepped up the teasing after I spent the weekend at Mrs. Martin's house when my brother Dave was born. But I only stayed there because my parents were close friends with the Martins.

The following week, Hank referred to me by the dreaded moniker. I ignored him until he repeated it in front of Sarah. I looked around. When I saw that Mrs. Martin and another teacher were nearby to break us up, I called Hank an unkind name and the fight was on. It lasted all of twenty seconds before the teachers stepped in. Exactly what I'd hoped for. The clash was quick, but it had released the tension in me.

However, a new emotion rushed in. I was dejected that I had let Mrs. Martin down. And added to that, I was pretty sure the preacher's kid was showing signs of being a hooligan.

Though I learned more about the three R's in my two years with Mrs. Martin than in all my other school years combined, she wasn't just about academics. She also had "talks" with the combined grades. Some were pleasant talks, like at Thanksgiving or Veterans Day, when she sought to inspire us with moving scenarios.

Then there were the talks that followed classroom conflicts—the ones that made us roll our eyes. I suppose Mrs. Martin meant them to be inspiring, too. She didn't design them to leave us stricken with guilt. Neither did she use them to build up a false sense of self-esteem. She trusted that they would instill balance in our lives and leave us wanting to be better people.

Following my skirmish with Hank, Mrs. Martin called an eye-rolling talk. This one had dual targets. It addressed our tendency to label others with unkind names, but it was also about us paying too much attention to what people say. Mrs. Martin always saw both sides of a situation.

She never mentioned bullying. She didn't lecture us on fighting or being passive onlookers. Instead, she talked about having kinder and more understanding hearts because that is where our behavior flows from. She explained it is what's inside us that makes us want to call other people names or causes us to be bothered when we get called names. To our astonishment, she said she sometimes had problems with that herself!

Hank and I had to sit with her during recess for a whole week. She was hitting us where it hurt. Though I could hardly believe it, I didn't get in trouble at home. Mrs. Martin talked to Dad, but they must have both realized that kids didn't always have the verbal skills to deal with conflict. They knew a fight was likely to break out at times. And Dad knew there were teachers like Mrs. Martin who would follow up our kerfuffles with character-building lessons.

Mrs. Martin taught me that the real battle we fight is within us. Fight that battle first, then take on the ones around us. Made a difference then, and it still does today.

That didn't mean Hank and I had everything patched up. We still made evil faces at each other during recess while Mrs. Martin wasn't watching.

~ ~ ~

THE SCHOOL YEAR PASSED and Sarah moved on to the seventh- and eighth-grade classroom. I already knew a lot of the sixth-grade material. That gave me time to notice the girls in my own class.

I had a weird way of showing I liked them. I would annoy them. Especially Michelle who sat in front of me. The desks butted up against each other, so it was easy to pester her. Since I wasn't all that creative, I used run-of-the-mill methods. I would tap her on the shoulder and act like it wasn't me. Or shake her desk with my feet.

Then one day I pulled her pigtail. She spun around in her seat so fast I thought she'd fly out of it. Her eyes burned laser holes in me. That was the moment I learned that young gentlemen don't pull young ladies' pigtails.

Michelle had finally had enough of my monkey business and decided to annoy me back. During cursive practice, she flipped her pigtails back on my desk. They lay curled over my writing tablet like two long black snakes. This was not just annoying. It was temptation beyond any level of resistance I had. I carefully lifted the lid of my desk and reached in for my scissors. There were serpents to behead.

I opened the scissors and rested the blades against one of the pigtails. Then I got Bruce's attention so he could witness the mighty slaying. Suddenly Michelle turned, saw what I was about to do, and let out a scream. Mrs. Martin swooped in and grabbed the weapon out of my hand. Besides losing my scissors, I got a huge talking to after school. More talk awaited me at home. This was serious. I was lucky I didn't start a feud between the Catholics and the Protestants in town.

Maybe I should explain. From what I could pick up, some Catholics thought the Methodists were going to hell, and vice versa. Michelle was from one of the few Catholic families in the area. Though we outnumbered them, they had the Pope and the president on their side. The two groups tried to stay polite to each other, but it might not have taken much beyond a slain pig-tail for hostilities to surface.

I never found out what happened behind the scenes, but Mrs. Martin must have smoothed things over with Michelle's parents. Then she did something unheard of. She switched our two seats —out of alphabetical order. Michelle was now in the position to pester *me* all day.

With her early use of affirmative action, Mrs. Martin showed a progressive side. Putting Michelle in the power seat would give one of the Catholics in class a chance to get even with the Protes-tants. Or maybe she moved me closer to her desk so she could better observe me reaping what I had so abundantly sown. Re-gardless of her reason, I began to realize there was something to that Bible verse that hung on her classroom wall. I prayed Michelle had already taken it to heart.

Chapter 5

Extreme Sports for All Seasons

HENRY WAS ABOUT the same age as the Cookie Lady. And he was just as cool. He lived two houses down from the parsonage on a dead-end road that ran almost parallel to SR 8. In the fall he burned his leaves on the road in front of his house.

A few houses beyond Henry lived the Long family. Kenny Long was three years younger than I was, but he and I often played together. Late one Saturday afternoon, he noticed a fresh pile of leaves on Henry's road. He rushed over to tell me, and we took off on our bikes. In less than a minute, we skidded to a stop in front of Henry's house.

Henry was just laying his rake down. He asked if we wanted to help him light the leaves. That was like asking Moe if he wanted to try out some new eye pokes on Curly. Of *course* we wanted to. He dipped two cattails into a can of oil and lit them. Then he handed one to each of us.

This was great. I had just gone from a ban on playing with matches to wielding an incendiary device given to me by an adult. Kenny and I had been selected for an important task. With great earnestness, we approached the pile from opposite sides and touched our torches to several places until Henry told us it was enough. Flames soon crackled through the dry leaves. Fragrant smoke ascended, marking the spot where history was being made, at least in our minds.

We watched as Henry repeatedly raked the untouched leaves on top of flames to keep the fire going. After a while, Kenny and I needed more to do than just watch, so still carrying our burning torches, we mounted our bikes and rode rings around the circle of fire. We had just enough wits about us to not run over Henry.

Our wits ran out, however, when our inner firebugs shouted, "More!" We answered back by riding our bikes *through* the burning leaves, screaming like banshees and trying to hold our feet up out of the flames. Each time, we scattered out the leaves. And each time, Henry raked them back in. Kenny's back tire was smoking after the third time, and the strings hanging from the bottom of my pants were singed.

Henry probably didn't mean for things to go that far, but as one thing led to another, he didn't stop us. Maybe he was putting himself in our smoldering shoes and knew just what a memory this would make. Or maybe there was more purpose to his non-action. Holding a lit torch while riding through flames took away my urge to play with matches. That day I realized that adult supervision wasn't so bad. Nothing would ever equal fire riding. Not even playing with carbide.

My clothes smelled like smoke at supper that night. Dad asked why and I didn't lie. (A recent lesson about lying hadn't worn off yet.) I was pleasantly surprised that neither Henry nor I got in trouble with Dad; I was hoping for at least one more good pile of leaves before winter hit.

~ ~ ~

AFTER THE SNOW STARTED FLYING, the boys, and an occasional girl, gravitated to Henry's hill with our sleds. His yard was steep and long. We often pulled our sleds clear up to the alley behind his house in order to create the longest course—about the length of a football field. Never mind that it began in a stretch of woods where we had to maneuver around a few trees before emerging. That just added to the excitement. Then we would pick up speed as we rocketed down the snow-covered slope.

Once on the hillside, we had two course options. One was a straight, gradual descent that joined Henry's driveway two-thirds of the way down, crossed his road, and ended in a small field. We practically always managed to stop our sleds there since the alternative would have been to continue on across SR 8. We could come up with enough dare-devil stunts without involving other vehicles.

Our other course veered right just above the driveway and went over a bank. We would fly several feet through the air before coming down in the middle of the road and continuing to the field. Though it came with more wow factor, it also came with more wear and tear on our sleds and bodies.

This should have been enough excitement, but adrenaline addiction sometimes led to the formation of sled trains. Everyone lay belly-down on their sleds and hooked their feet onto the metal cross-bar of the sled behind them. A train might have as many as ten sleds. The engine got to choose whether we took the driveway or the bank. The bank provided more thrills, but the leader risked having multiple sleds come down on him when the flying train landed. It was safest to be in the back for either course, but especially for the bank. Our parents thought we wore several thick layers for protection against the cold. Really, we wanted protection from cuts and contusions.

One time Kenny showed up early with a large watering can and began sprinkling the course with water. When I got there, we made many more trips back and forth to his house until we had iced the entire course. By the time the rest of the guys arrived, we had an extreme track by any measure. If we took the straight course, we had to work extra hard to stop from sliding onto SR 8. If we chose to go over the bank, we sometimes cleared Henry's road altogether and landed in the field. The fast ice robbed us of any control. We landed nose first, on our sides, or even on our backs underneath our sleds—any way but pretty.

Mere supersonic speed and bone-crushing sled trains did not satisfy Jerry's oldest brother, though. Carl was two years older than us and a little crazy even by our standards. If we had dared him to jump out the window, he likely would have gone a story higher to do so. One day Carl decided to conquer the hill while standing on his sled. When he reached the driveway, he took the bank. We heard him scream as he sailed through the air. His feet left the sled and only reconnected with it briefly when it touched down. At once he went somersaulting across the field with his sled bouncing behind. A few minutes later, he returned to the top dazed and smiling, ready to go again. Not to be outdone, a few of us attempted the feat, only to dot the hillside with our sprawled-out bodies. We remained outdone by Carl.

The only thing that could have made Sled Hill better would have been for Henry to have a pile of burning leaves at the bottom to plow through.

I had several noteworthy crashes on Sled Hill, but none like the one on Bike Hill the following summer.

~ ~ ~

I GOT A NEW BIKE for my twelfth birthday. It had something to do with the tires on my old one aging prematurely due to excessive heat. The new one was candy apple red with chrome fenders. I soon outfitted it with all the important accessories: a battery-powered horn, a headlight, a speedometer, and real coontails that streamed from the handlebars. It was ready for Bike Hill.

Bike Hill was the best hill around, sanctioned, albeit reluctantly, by our parents thanks to how little traffic it saw. The quarter-mile section of country road started out steeply at the top so we could immediately get up a good speed. Then it settled into a more gradual descent with curves right and left. They weren't sharp, but they required some braking if we didn't want to fly off into a hayfield, or worse, the woods.

I made several trips to Bike Hill by myself to try out my new machine. It was a dandy. As hard as I had tried to pedal my old one clear to the top, I had to settle on pushing it the last fifty yards or so. With my new ride, I had the ability to pedal all the way up. And it was fast going down—35 mph before I reached the curves.

I rode to Jerry's one day to see if he could go to the Hill. I wanted to show off what my bike could do. He wasn't home, but Crazy Carl was there. And Carl was always in the mood for Bike Hill. I knew it was a huge mistake, but off we rode.

When we reached the top of the hill, Carl had the wildest look in his eyes I had ever seen. No doubt he thought he could beat my new bike to the bottom. I hadn't told him I could do 35 on it. Would he ever be surprised.

We began the descent, and I took the lead. Soon I heard some crazed yelping and turned to see Carl closing the gap. He came right up beside me, trying to see how close he could get. He got close all right. His pedal caught in my front wheel and removed every—and I mean *every*—spoke.

The experience was surreal. A long second passed before forward momentum gave way to downward force. Bikes and bodies skidded across the gravel shoulder into a field. It was the wreck of all wrecks on Bike Hill.

It turned out that Carl and I both reached the bottom of the hill at the same time—pushing and carrying what was left of our machines. I wore my front wheel around my neck. Blood and bits of gravel covered our faces and arms, and our clothes were tattered.

Carl said he was sorry, but he wore a grin that wouldn't quit. That just made me madder. I yelled at him, but then I felt bad about it. After all, Carl was just being Carl. If I was smarter, I wouldn't have gone to Bike Hill with him, so I guess a lot of it was my fault.

It would be a long time before I had wheels again. And this escapade meant a trip to Dr. Trimnell's for both of us. I felt only a little guilty when I dared Carl to ask for the largest needle.

~ ~ ~

WE OBVIOUSLY HAD A KNACK for escalating the danger level of our outdoor sports. The school arena was no different. Though Mrs. Martin structured most recess periods with supervised games such as kickball, dodgeball, and statue tag, once a month we had a free day in which things became a little more perilous.

Our chosen activities on these days were fairly predictable. Many students would sprint to one side of the playground to form lines for a wrist-bruising game of Red Rover. On the other side, dodgeball would start up. This game was dangerous enough to satisfy us when supervised, but now we could take it up a notch with harder throws and kicks. Sometimes the two games even morphed into one; we could have a dodgeball slamming us as we tried to ram through the human walls. If all of that became too violent for us, we could settle for a jump off the wildly spinning merry-go-round or bail out of a high-flying swing.

We all looked forward to free day. Mrs. Martin was willing to let us hurt ourselves if we were that stupid, and she had a first aid kit handy that she was quite adept at using. She appointed the kids who broke what few rules existed to clean erasers *on recess time.*

Not everyone was into the roughhousing. There were always a handful of students who could be found perched on the wooden fence that edged the playground, preferring to fill the spectator role.

~ ~ ~

OUR DARING FEATS on, and off, the playground toughened us up. We learned to duck quickly, hang on tightly, and land on our feet, even though we experienced some bumps, bruises, and loss of blood in the process.

Since those days, I've gotten the extreme sports out of my system. Now it's my wife Bonnie who's got the bug. We went ziplining a few years back at her request. She's working on getting me into a skydiving wind tunnel the next time we go to Pigeon Forge. She's even begun talking up a white-water rafting trip.

I'll do that for her, but lately I prefer to sit on the fence and just watch the violence.

Chapter 6

Free-Range Trick-or-Treating

IT SNOWED TWO INCHES ON HALLOWEEN. I was happier than a grin on a jack-o'-lantern when Mrs. Martin assured us that snow would not cancel trick-or-treating that night.

The roads had been bare when I parked my bike in the rack before school began. By mid-morning, though, when we went out for recess, a blanket of snow covered the playground. Our excitement at this early taste of winter, not to mention it was Halloween, caused us to dart around like squirrels on caffeine. Mrs. Martin had to use her first-aid kit three times on us. To say the least, it was hard to focus on multiplication tables and the War of 1812 when we got back in the classroom. By the time we had all vacated the building after the last bell, Mrs. Martin was probably questioning her chosen profession.

I rode my bike straight home, resisting the temptation to test it out on the first snow of the year. I still had work to do on my costume for the big night. The idea had come to me the Sunday before when Dad had tried to soften the hearts of the congregation on giving: "Give to the needy. The Bible tells us, 'you shall not harden your heart or shut your hand against your poor brother, but you shall open your hand to him.'" I hoped this included candy. The kicker was, "Give to him who begs from you." That's when I decided to dress like a bum. And, though Dad didn't ask me to, I'd report to him afterward whether the folks were complying with the sacred scriptures.

Mom usually took us begging, but she wasn't excited about going out in the snow that night. She arranged for one of Marge's relatives to escort Paula and Lloyd. It thrilled me when she said I could roam the town on my own. Between the two of them, Dad and Mom were acquainted with practically everyone in town by then, so they had no safety concerns about the neighbors in our quiet little burg. I planned on taking full advantage of this new freedom and not hang anywhere near my siblings.

Strict town protocol kept kids from knocking on doors before six o'clock. I asked Mom if I could leave a little early so I could get to the farthest house and be on the doorstep at starting time. She said it was up to me if I wanted to freeze. Then she smiled and told me how pitiful I looked. That's exactly what I wanted to hear. She had done great at picking out clothes for me at the thrift store, and I had finished the job by ripping them up.

Dad and Mom had a vested interest in us doing well on Beggar's Night. Every year they both went through our candy to pick five treats from each bag. Their excuse for the inspection and confiscation was that they needed to remove candy that might contain hard, dangerous objects, such as almonds and walnuts. I thought it strange that on this one day of the year they always became more concerned about their children's teeth.

My goal for the night was to collect enough candy so that after Dad and Mom took their shares, I would have enough left to last until Thanksgiving. I'd gotten word that everyone gave pies to the preacher then. When those ran out, I knew Mom would bake Christmas cookies. They would last until we raked in a plethora of sweets from the school and church Christmas parties and from our stockings. So if I had a good night of begging, I shouldn't have a deficiency in the sugar food group for two months.

~ ~ ~

A TIME-CONSCIOUS VAGRANT rang the first doorbell at precisely six o'clock. Despite my punctuality, things started out slowly. I got two popcorn balls at the Thompson house and a huge apple, not even candied, at the next one. I thanked the treaters through a painted-on smile while hoping the fare would get better. With a hundred houses to go, popcorn balls took up too much room and apples were too heavy. Besides, if it wasn't processed sugar, I didn't want it.

At the third house, two pennies dropped into my bag. I began to doubt my choice of costume. Maybe the townspeople thought bums didn't eat candy and they could satisfy us with small change. I shivered as the wind blew through the holes I'd torn in my pant legs.

My fortune changed at the Mooneys'. I hit pay dirt with a large Pay Day and a quarter. The Mooneys didn't even go to Dad's church. Maybe they had heard a better compassion sermon at the Assembly of God.

At the next house I got a five-pack of assorted-flavored Nik-L Nips plus wax lips and teeth. The Burgess family had been at church the week before and must have paid attention to the preacher. This was good research for my report to Dad. A giant Hollywood candy bar plopped into my sack at the next stop.

For the rest of the night, there was a hole in the streets of heaven. Into my pillowcase fell glorious treasures: Zeroes, Milkshakes, Big Times, One Hundred Grands, Milky Ways, Necco Wafers, Atomic Fireballs, Tootsie Roll Pops, Pixie Stix, Candy Buttons, Fizzies, Fruit Stripe Gum, Good and Plenty, and Sugar Daddies. I would have pitched the Neapolitan Coconut candy bar into the bushes, but I hoped Mom would pick it as one of her choices. I'd even throw in the apple for free if she did.

I slipped the candy cigarettes into my pocket for safe keeping. Dad had given up his Winstons when he was born again, and he wouldn't stand for *any* kind of cigarettes to touch our lips. I did leave the licorice pipes in the bag, thinking he might allow them as a safe alternative.

Only about ten houses did not open their doors to trick-or-treaters. At one of them, I saw lights and heard a radio. It was way too cold to soap their windows, so I grabbed a handful of corn kernels from my pocket and flung them against the large front window. Then I ran like a scared rabbit. It probably wouldn't teach them not to hold out, but it was fun.

The absolute scariest house was right on SR 8 on the south side of town. To get to the treats, I had to get past five creepy straw-stuffed monsters. The house sat just beyond the sidewalk. With no front yard, the monsters congregated on the wooden porch that ran the length of the house. I saw Jerry and his brothers nearby and decided it might be time to become sociable and approach the porch of horrors in numbers.

Mr. and Mrs. Weatherbee loved to scare the willies out of us kids. One of their creatures had a large pumpkin head with eerily glowing orange eyes. And Frankenstein's long arms were permanently outstretched as though he were about to steal my candy, or worse, grab *me*. Two of the other monsters just towered over us, their size alone being enough to scare us silly.

The devil was the most sinister. He stood right next to the door, so there was no way to avoid him. An evil sounding voice seemed to come right out of his mouth. As I approached the door, I heard him say, "I'm going to get you someday . . . even if you *are* a PK." I nearly dropped my bag. *Could he know about the cigarettes in my pocket?*

The window directly behind the devil was slightly open, and I thought I saw Mr. Weatherbee peering out of the darkness on the other side of the screen. I suspected he was the voice of the devil, expressing hidden sentiments. Mr. Weatherbee was generally nice to me, but he did often comment about how uncompromising the churches and preachers in town were. No doubt the strictness was a necessary countermeasure to Satan's yearly appearance on the town's thoroughfare.

We dared Carl to knock on the door, and of course he did. An ugly witch appeared. We assumed it had to be Mrs. Weatherbee. She was normally a very pleasant lady, but not on Halloween. With long pointed red fingernails, she grabbed a huge handful of penny candy for each of us. I opened my bag wide to avoid getting scratched. Her screechy laugh gave me goosebumps. This was a big night for the Weatherbees. The kids all loved it too, but we didn't realize it until after we stepped off the porch and our insides stopped shaking.

The next stop was the church. Betty Wilson, our youth leader, was busy setting out refreshments for us in the basement. Her brother-in-law Fred was waiting outside with his wagon and tractor to give rides. He had piled it high with loose hay. Because of the cold temperature, he had covered the wagon with a large piece of canvas that hung over the side rails. We left our candy in the church with Mrs. Wilson. It seemed a little suspicious that her brother-in-law was the one whisking us away. Just in case they were in cahoots with each other, I rigged my bag so I would be able to tell if anyone tampered with it.

We rode through the side streets of town. If we wanted to look out, we had to lift the canvas. We preferred to keep the cold air out though. After a half hour of sugared up kids wrestling and getting hay in our clothes, we returned to the church for hot chocolate and cookies. After that, I was ready to get home and take inventory of my stash. I thought this might be my biggest haul ever.

Lloyd and Paula entered the house soon after I did and dumped their bags on the living room floor. My eyes got big when I saw their abundant take. They hadn't gone to as many houses as I had; their youth and cuteness must have loosened the coffers and ramped up the giving spirit that Dad had preached about. Well, at least I had more than they did. The hard work of a bum had triumphed.

Like every year, I sorted my goodies into three piles. In pile one was the good stuff. I stared at the huge mountain of deliciousness, one that would thrill any ten-year-old bum. Pile two contained Neapolitan Coconut and other candy I *might* eat when the candy from pile one ran out and I became desperate for sugar.

I reserved pile three for the rejects, things like apples and popcorn balls that would likely never be consumed unless I could talk Mom or Dad into picking from it. But that probably wasn't going to happen since we all had the same sugar genes.

My first solo trick-or-treat had been a great success, for me and for Dad. I was well stocked till the new year arrived. And I could report to Dad that his parishioners had taken his sermon to heart—and offer a strong recommendation that he break out the same message every year about this time.

Chapter 7

Stifled Emotions

IN MY FAMILY and those of my friends, parents were the main characters on stage. Children had only supporting roles. And in that pre-emoji era, our parents did not encourage us to express our feelings or opinions, unless they were in harmony with the household script.

I grew up thinking that if I had any problem with family policy, I was an ungrateful child. When I felt bad about something, I did not complain around Dad. Maybe to Mom a little, but I had to be careful there. She might tell Dad. Then a bad feeling could plummet to something much worse.

Parents in Tippecanoe seemed to give a neighbor's kid more slack than they did their own, maybe even a little sympathy. So if a kid did any grouching, he did it to someone else's parents. Jerry must have needed a lot of sympathy because he sure was at our house a lot. It shocked me to see him get away with complaining to my dad. I wanted to complain about that, but I knew better.

Two TV shows debuted in the fall of 1960, however, that starred Dads with a tender spot that could occasionally be manipulated by their kids. Andy Griffith began beaming from TV sets at 9:30 p.m. every Monday. Since my parents had just recently extended my bedtime to nine o'clock, I decided a visit to Mayberry would have to wait until next year. The other program, though, began at nine. A faint hope welled up in me that I could get an extra extension, just for Thursday nights, to see what Steve Douglas was stirring up on *My Three Sons*.

The buzz at school was that Mr. Douglas, though strict at times, held family meetings in which his sons had a say in important matters. The boys could complain at home, and even get a little sympathy once in a while. Since this idea was almost scandalous, Jerry and I kept our voices low when we talked about the Douglases. I was pretty sure Dad had not heard about the radical ideas the new show was encouraging or he would have preached about it.

It took a few days for me to work up the nerve to talk to Dad about extending my bedtime—again. In the meantime, I modeled Jerry's gooey-good behavior around them. And to prove myself worthy of last month's extension, I had been popping up out of bed in the morning like Wonder Bread from a new toaster. However, like our aging appliance, I couldn't keep that up much longer. I needed to act before the coils stopped glowing.

One evening, I crossed the threshold into a place where wimpy kids dared not enter: Dad's study. He was putting the finishing touches on Sunday's sermon. I could only hope he would be impressed that his eldest son had the guts to go for another new bedtime so soon.

Don't look like you are moping. I made eye contact.

But before I could get anything past my vocal cords, Dad spewed out my six least favorite words: "Are you mad, sick, or tired?" The coils went cold.

~ ~ ~

THAT QUESTION, which Dad had pulled out of his hat a few times before, drove me insane on every level. The first time I said I was mad, he told me to "straighten up." That discouraged any more self-diagnoses of the anger malady. So I really had only two options.

If I admitted to being sick, that meant I had to pick a cure, my choices being castor oil, Dr. Trimnell's needles, or an immediate ticket to bed with no passing Go. Even though I hated bed, it was my no-brainer choice if I was sick.

My safest option was to declare tiredness, though it had its drawbacks, too. It also involved banishment to my room for a nap—unless I was in the middle of a chore, in front of a plate of liver and broccoli, or getting ready for church. Sometimes it earned me the nap *and* an earlier bedtime that night. To avoid the double dose treatment, I quickly learned to say I was "just a *little* tired."

The hands on Dad's desk clock paused, waiting for my answer. I ran through my choices. I wasn't mad. Well, maybe a little at hearing Dad's question, but I wasn't going to go there. I wasn't quite sick. My stomach felt as if it could easily turn in that direction, but that would do nothing to help my cause. And there was no way I was going to say I was tired when I was about to ask for a later bedtime.

Just then, right there in the preacher's study, a miracle happened. A thought came down from heaven in my time of great need. In one super-long breath I blurted out, "Dad, I'm not mad, sick, *or* tired. I just wanna stay up later on Thursday to see *My Three Sons*."

"Next Thursday night? Sure."

That was almost too easy. Though it wasn't all I'd wanted, I decided to take what was given and not do anything to mess it up. I popped out of the study with a quick "Thanks, Dad," feeling very accomplished at my newfound negotiating skills.

~ ~ ~

THE FOLLOWING WEDNESDAY, I sat in school waiting for dismissal. We would get out an hour early because the next day was Thanksgiving. As I stared at the second motionless clock in less than a week, the gears in my head started turning. I realized that this Thursday I would be allowed to stay up anyway since there was no school Friday. Dad had tricked me. He knew exactly what he was doing when he granted the bedtime extension for only this week.

I felt mad, sick, and tired all at once. When Mrs. Martin asked for volunteers to share what they were thankful for, I barely heard her. I was not full of thanks as I thought of having to work up the nerve all over again next week to ask for a *regular* Thursday night bedtime extension.

I suffered through sharing time. When the bell rang, I sulked home. The rest of the day, I stayed outside or at the neighbors' as much as I could so Dad and Mom wouldn't see me moping.

The next morning, I awoke to the scrumptious smells of Thanksgiving. Then Dad broke out the baseball gloves for a game of catch with me. Before we ate, everyone in the family shared what they were thankful for. By the time we sat down to dinner,

I forgot to be mad. I couldn't hide a big smile as I gobbled up turkey, stuffing, and pumpkin pie.

At nine o'clock, the whole family gathered to watch *My Three Sons*. It wasn't what the kids at school had it cracked up to be. In fact, all three of the Douglas boys got in trouble that episode. There was no family meeting where they could tell their side. And they didn't get any sympathy. I didn't need my parents watching this. I decided I wouldn't pursue a later bedtime for a while.

The experience wasn't a total flop though. My off-the-script answer to Dad had shaken things up. Basically, I had put an end to his "mad, sick, or tired" ploy.

I didn't escape unscathed. I sometimes still have difficulty expressing my feelings, especially negative ones. But I harbor no ill will about how my parents raised me. Dad probably got the saying from his dad, who got it from his dad, who . . . Well, you get the picture. And I just happened to be the one destined to break that particular family habit.

Not that I'm complaining, mind you.

Chapter 8

Playing with Eddie

I MET EDDIE the day my family moved to Tippecanoe. He showed up at my house on his bike to check out the moving van. In the unfiltered language of a ten-year-old boy, Eddie told me his dad had given him permission to ride over to see the new "holy rollers" in town. But he'd just better watch we didn't try to baptize him.

This took me by surprise; I was brand new to being a preacher's kid. But I had been excited about our move from the beginning and was happy to have made a friend so soon. It didn't take long for us to discover we would be in the same grade in the fall.

Dad took a walk the next day to get acquainted with the town. He met Eddie's father in the hardware store. When he introduced himself and offered his hand, Mr. Singleton warily shook it as if he might be stricken by the Spirit.

"Those are workingman's hands," Dad commented.

"Steel mill."

"I used to be in the lumber business. Do you go to church?" Dad didn't do much beating around the bush.

Neither did Mr. Singleton. "Never. Too many holier-than-thous in this town."

"Fish?"

"Uh . . . yeah. Hunt, too. We have a sportsman's club near the lake. Do some drinking there, too."

"Sounds like a man's kind of place."

"Why . . . yes, Reverend. There are some temperance ladies who give us a hard time though."

"They can get overzealous, I suppose."

"Sure can, Reverend. I'm a sinner and I like it. I don't like church and preachers, but, you know, I will treat you like a man should."

"I'm a little hard on sinners sometimes, Mr. Singleton, but if you want to come over and talk about fishing, I've got a few tales."

"Call me Herman. And let me know if you need help moving in."

"Will do, Herman. Thanks."

After an awkward beginning, men from two different worlds made their peace. They settled on mutual respect despite their differing lifestyles. I saw firsthand what agreeing to disagree looks like.

~ ~ ~

I MUST HAVE HAD A TARGET ON ME when I played with Eddie. That first year, I experienced a series of accidents at his hands that possibly strained our fathers' relationship more than it did ours.

The first incident occurred in the fall and took place in the tiny front yard of the parsonage. On one side was the church building. Along the front was a sidewalk, the only thing separating us from a bank down to SR 8. The other side of the yard was edged with a block wall that provided a four-foot drop-off to the concrete drive below. It was a stupid place to play any kind of running game. Especially with Eddie. I liked Eddie. He wasn't malicious, but he liked to play rough. I usually came home from our escapades with the lion's share of bumps and bruises.

Our game started out as tag, but somehow morphed into tackle. One of Eddie's hits sent me headfirst over the wall onto the driveway. All my weight came down on my left arm. I screamed in agony until Dad came out of the house. He rushed me to Twin City Hospital where X-rays revealed a fractured ulna. The doctor fitted me with a cast from above my elbow down to my fingers. Dad waited until the drive home to ask what had happened. I told him. He didn't ask any more questions.

As the pain subsided, I realized how cool looking my cast was. I would be the talk of my class. I'd get everyone to sign it. This wouldn't be so bad. During the evening, however, my cast started feeling tight. I kept telling Dad and Mom how uncomfortable my arm was. I was their first offspring to break a bone, so they weren't sure what to do. They finally decided that what I was experiencing was probably normal.

The pain returned and escalated through the night. By morning, my fingers were blue. Dad and Mom rethought their "probably normal" diagnosis, and Dad took me back to the hospital.

My arm had swollen and needed more room. The doctor split my cast its entire length and wrapped an elastic bandage around it to hold it together. "No new cast?" I asked in disbelief. No, he told me, this would work just fine and save the price of a new cast. But how could my friends sign a bandage? Suddenly, I hated my cast.

In a few days, the bandage got dirty and that is what I was stuck with for six weeks. During this time, I was hesitant about getting too near Eddie. After his father made him apologize, we did play together once in a while.

When my cast came off, all the skin underneath was pale and wrinkly from the water that had found its way underneath the cast for the past several weeks. My arm and hand looked like one of the freshly molted crabs we often saw in the stream. Dad took me straight to school, just in time for afternoon recess. I chased classmates with my pruny arm extended and my hand mimicking the pincer of a crab, trying to catch them in my claw. They called me The Crab for the rest of the day.

~ ~ ~

THE NEXT INCIDENT didn't break any bones or draw any blood, but it was twice as scary. By winter, I was playing with Eddie regularly again. On Christmas afternoon, I went over to his house. He lived halfway between Henry and Kenny. His backyard was home to one of the best climbing trees in town. I made my way up about twenty feet to get some altitude to launch my new rubber band balsa wood glider. Eddie had gotten a new BB gun that morning and was looking for targets. My eyelid was one of the first things he shot with it—and it would be the last.

I fell from my perch screaming. When Eddie's dad, who was up the hill splitting wood, heard me yelling, he raced down, ax still in hand. He pulled my hand away from my eye. Not seeing any damage, he then got the story out of Eddie. Anger spewed from him, permeating the entire yard. He grabbed Eddie's new gun and broke it over his knee like it was a twig. Then he sent me home. I couldn't exit fast enough.

While listening to my account, Dad and Mom examined my eye. It was red and puffy, but they found nothing requiring medical attention. The fate of Eddie's gun gave them some satisfaction. But now they were as leery as I was about me playing with Eddie.

Things quieted down for the next few months, but the shooting was not forgotten. A shaky, unspoken truce existed between our families.

~ ~ ~

ON A SATURDAY AFTERNOON, Eddie, Jerry, Bruce, and I raced for the playground behind the school. It served as the airfield anytime we flew our model airplanes. I had a new control line gas-powered plastic trainer plane that was making its maiden flight that day.

Just flying our planes wasn't enough for us. We had all-out war. While one of us flew his plane, the others tried to shoot it out of the sky. Our weapons were relatively harmless slingshots and marbles. If we ran out of marbles, we picked up stones for ammo. We hadn't tried BB guns at this point. Three of us didn't own one yet, and Eddie had only two useless halves.

Eddie and Jerry got the engine going with only minor finger damage. Bruce gave the OK signal. The takeoff was shaky; I almost plowed my new plane into the ground the first few times around the field. Then I started to get the hang of it, and the craft steadied out. I nodded my head to signal the enemy to begin firing their missiles. The marbles flew wildly. One shot finally made a direct hit, but the marble bounced off and the plane continued undaunted on its mission.

It was great—until *I* took a direct hit, in the forehead. I didn't know I would need a helmet that day. Taking out the pilot is one way to down a plane, but no one had informed me that the rules of our game had changed to permit that. I fell to the ground and so did my plane.

I never knew who got me. Jerry and Bruce were glowing with innocence while Eddie was reeking of guilt. But then, Eddie always looked blameworthy when something happened, whether he was the culprit or not. Just observing him and knowing the history he and I had together would bring a unanimous guilty verdict from a jury even before they left the box to deliberate . . . and even if his grandma was among the jurors.

I knew who my parents would suspect, especially Mom, so I didn't want to tell them I was hurt. I was just relieved my plane had miraculously survived the crash. However, I couldn't hide the bruise spreading over my right eye and up to my hairline.

When I got home, I tried to steer the possibility of blame to Jerry or Bruce, not from malice but to protect Eddie. He needed someone on his side. Mom said something about history repeating itself. She was obviously upset, but Dad portrayed calm for her sake. He reminded her that I had been a willing participant. I knew he was mad though. I had seen that vein popping out on his forehead more than a few times before.

Dad said he would talk to Herman. Man to man. They would work this out. Next thing I knew, Dad was headed to Eddie's house, dragging me and my ugly bruise behind him.

Dad rang the doorbell. Through the front window, we could see Mr. Singleton get up from his favorite chair and come to the door. He asked us in and offered Dad a beer. Dad declined, though this was a situation which well could have driven the preacher to drink.

I stood beside Dad as he filled Mr. Singleton in on the events that had transpired at the school grounds a short time before. Then Eddie's dad called his son out of his room and questioned him. Eddie said marbles were flying everywhere, but he insisted it wasn't his that got me.

"What are you going to do, Preacher? Sue me?"

"No, Herman, I don't do things that way. The Bible teaches us to try to settle disputes in other ways."

"Well then, I guess you'd like to punch me in the nose."

"I've thought about it."

"I guess you know I'll have to punch you back, preacher or not."

"Yeah, maybe we should try talking instead. Besides, maybe it wasn't even Eddie who did it."

We all looked at Eddie. You could hardly see his freckles with the guilt written all over his face.

"I don't know about that," said Herman. "Sure you don't want a beer, Preacher?"

"Don't tempt me, Herman. You know those temperance gals."

"OK. Let's sit down. You boys go outside. No, on second thought, you'd better stay right here."

Dad and Mr. Singleton talked through the situation while Eddie and I listened from across the room. With only a 33 percent chance that Eddie had launched the errant marble, they decided they couldn't fairly lay the blame on him. And they both believed that whatever had happened, it was most certainly a case of friendly fire. After Dad agreed to talk with the other boys and their fathers about slingshot etiquette, Dad and Mr. Single-ton shook hands. On the way home, I received a personal tutorial on the proper use of my own slingshot.

Dad, like most folks in Tippecanoe, didn't believe in playing the litigation card. He was for people working together to find solutions to their problems. The results were way better. And a lot less expensive than hiring lawyers.

That left more money to cover doctor bills—which was a good thing if you ever played with Eddie.

Chapter 9

Mishandled Fame

PEOPLE IN SMALL TOWNS are hungry for heroes. Lady Luck smiled on me one day, and I found myself in a position to satisfy their appetites.

It began early one spring morning. All my friends were either still in bed or warming up their TVs so they wouldn't miss the opening theme for the Saturday broadcast of *Captain Kangaroo*. I was out well before the cartoons started, mindlessly biking around town.

I stopped to admire the new body of water in the field across SR 8. Stillwater Creek had overflowed its banks the week before, submerging the field and stopping just short of the road. Though the water had now receded, a small pond remained.

I was about to head home when I noticed a colossal disturbance in the water. It had to be created by at least a minisub, I thought; I had suspected that foreign spies patrolled Stillwater Creek. Or maybe it was a baby whale. Both possibilities seemed equally plausible to my young imagination. I would just have to catch up with the Captain next Saturday.

I dropped my bike on the spot and raced across the road. Now that the skid marks had disappeared, I was allowed to cross by myself. As I sloshed through the muddy field, I didn't find any subs or whales, but I did discover the largest carp I had ever seen. They were splashing wildly in water less than a foot deep.

I rode home and got the wheelbarrow. It was heavy for me even when empty, but now adrenaline was powering it down the road and across the field. I jumped in the water and wrestled out five giant fish. I called on all my sugar reserves and managed to awkwardly push the load back home.

Mrs. Wilson lived across the road from the parsonage. She happened to be outside and hurried over to see what I was hauling. She eagerly asked where I caught the fish. I couldn't think how to answer her, so I just pointed toward Stillwater Creek. She insisted on calling the *Freeport Press* to send over a reporter, sure that this had to be some kind of fishing first for the town.

It's hard to argue with a youth leader. And I *did* catch the carp . . . kind of. I figured it wouldn't hurt to hold back some details. Even from Mrs. Wilson. This was different from lying about the carbide. I wasn't actually saying any untrue words. Bring on the press! Meanwhile, I dashed to the basement and changed into dry clothes. Most people don't get that muddy fishing with a pole.

As the news spread, more townsfolk gathered around my wheelbarrow, marveling at the spectacle. Henry was there, but he wasn't marveling. His eyes shifted back and forth between the flopping fish and me. I was pretty sure that he knew how I "caught" them. I was close to fessing up when Dad came out and acted as if his son brought a wheelbarrow full of fish home every day. Then the reporter pulled into the driveway. I felt as trapped as the carp in the field.

The reporter told me to run and grab my pole. I was relieved that I was able to find it quickly. I smiled while posing beside my catch and tried to avoid eye contact with Henry. As I stood with pole in hand, surrounded by people who proudly acknowledged my fishing superskills, I didn't see how it could hurt to give them the hero they wanted. Anyway, I was starting to believe the fish story myself.

The fame of my angling skills waned after a few months. In a way, it was a relief. All that time, I had dreaded someone asking me if I had actually used a pole. They didn't, so I never had to lie. In the back of my mind, though, I wondered if everyone suspected the truth but didn't want to spoil a good story. Not much happened in town that was newsworthy.

~ ~ ~

EVERYBODY IN TOWN burned their trash. We burned ours next door behind the church in an enclosure of cement blocks stacked three high. The job was always mine if I was available. My parents never had to tell me twice because it was the only time they let me use matches.

One day, the wind kept blowing my matches out. When I finally got a fire started, my adversary turned helpful by whipping up a strong flame. A major part of my job was to make sure the fire didn't get out of hand and spread outside the blocks, especially during the dry season. I took my role as fire chief seriously.

For some reason long forgotten, though, I left my post and ran back to my basement. While inside, something distracted me. My thoughts didn't return to the outside world until I heard the siren wailing at the firehouse a block away. *Cool! Wonder where the fire is.*

I didn't have to wonder long. By the time I emerged from the basement, firemen were battling the flames on the hillside behind the church. I got as close as I could to get a better look. Queasiness invaded my stomach and dizziness swirled in my head. Needing to escape from the incriminating scene, I staggered toward the house.

Oh, would there ever be music to face . . . or maybe not. I thought perhaps I could turn my light-headedness into something productive. Before I reached my house, I crumpled to the ground in a feigned faint. An annoying voice in my head told me I was a coward. I responded with, "So, what's your point?" I silenced the voice like I planned to silence the music and basked in the attention from concerned neighbors as they administered first aid and love. After all, I was the town's young fishing champ, wasn't I?

When I "came to," I noticed Henry among the concerned, but not among those dispensing TLC. He stood quietly at a short distance, his eyes fixed on me with a knowing look. I didn't want to know what he knew.

I did get in trouble for leaving the fire, but Mom stepped in on my behalf. She reminded Dad that I had already been through a lot, and she didn't want me to faint again. Surprisingly, Dad went light. And that afternoon, he stacked the blocks up another couple of rows.

~ ~ ~

A FEW DAYS LATER I saw Henry working in his garden, retying tomato plants to their stakes. With his long nose and disheveled hair, he made a convincing scarecrow. I joined him, grabbed the hoe, and acted as though I knew what I was doing.

We talked a while about making torches and burning leaves. I was careful to avoid the topic of burning hillsides. We touched on other areas of Henry's expertise. Then I brought up something that had been bothering me for the past month. "Henry, what's a lie?"

"What do *you* think?" he said, answering my question with a question. He must have learned that technique from my dad.

"It's when you say things that aren't true."

There was no response from Henry. We worked in silence. After a few minutes, I felt compelled to confess my lie about playing with carbide.

Henry smiled. "Yes, I heard about that one."

That was a shocker. I tried to figure out who might have told him. Surely not Bruce; he wouldn't want to get me in trouble. It was probably Dad. Henry seldom came to church, but I'd see him and Dad talking many a time, often over large juicy tomatoes or cucumbers.

While Henry was giving me a hoeing lesson, I spotted Jerry and Eddie riding their bikes out on SR 8.

"Henry, can I yell down to the guys to come up? They might want a tomato." We all loved Henry's tomatoes, and I was feeling especially generous that day with his bounty.

"No. Let's hide so they won't see us," he said as he stepped behind the corn, motioning for me to follow. "Hurry. I don't want them eating any tomatoes today."

For Henry to move quickly was surprise enough, but to hide from the boys like that was incredible. We hunkered down till the guys pedaled on past.

"That was a close one," he said when they were out of sight. "I need to save some tomatoes for canning."

"But why don't you just tell Eddie and Jerry that if they ask for one?"

"Well, I could," he said, scratching his chin. "But I decided to take the easy way out. If they don't ask, I don't have to tell them. Don't you think that's OK?"

Henry's eyes were gentle as they searched deep inside me. It was the same look I had seen on his face by the burning hillside, and also when the reporter was taking my picture. Then his face blurred, and five giant carp appeared in my mind, staring at me from a wheelbarrow, their big round mouths opening and closing. They were saying, "Liar . . . liar . . . liar."

"Better get yourself a tomato so you don't go fainting on me," Henry said with a wink.

~ ~ ~

I UNDERSTAND NOW why the preacher talked often and passionately with Henry. He probably got a few sermon ideas from my wise friend, including one on the importance of being honest. I know I caught that lesson one afternoon while fishing for tomatoes in his garden.

And that's the whole truth, even if you didn't ask.

Chapter 10

The Flyswatter and Other Corporal Punishments

MY PARENTS were not the most consistent disciplinarians. Especially Mom. Most of the time, I could do whatever I wanted as long as she was happy with me. That meant doing the thoughtful things that moms deserve: make or buy something special for Mother's Day, her birthday, and Christmas; leave my muddy shoes in the garage before entering the house; and thank her once in a while for everything she did.

I was an expert on knowing when to interrupt to get permission to do things. One good time to approach Mom was when she was with her friends. Another promising time was when a commercial came on between segments of *Perry Mason*. Her favorite show made her feel so good she'd say yes to almost anything.

With Mom, even no was not always no. She would often give in if I bugged her enough. If that didn't work, I turned on the whining. And, in the extremely hard cases, I pumped in a little attitude. That was a dangerous undertaking, though, because too much might make her mad.

If I pushed her past her tipping point, out came the flyswatter. Not one of those flimsy things, but one that could deliver quite a sting. Since I could outrun her, I was safe as long as I didn't get trapped in a corner.

What would bring my victory run to a screeching halt, however, was hearing her say, "Wait till your father comes home." Those words instantly birthed fear in me. My only hope at that point was that I could do enough penance with my tears and blubbering that she would revoke the threat. But if she followed through, that hope was smashed into nothing even remotely recognizable, like a fly on our front window that didn't see it coming. Dad would then handle the deed. And not with the swatter.

I played the game, and I knew the penalties. I could have just taken a few hits through the pants with the swatter. But I shared with the flies a survival mentality that urged me to dodge imminent danger. Too bad for me that, unlike the flies, something worse could be waiting beyond the flyswatter.

~ ~ ~

I WAS THANKFUL that Mom did not play the Dad card often. Dad's modus operandi was to apply the "Board of Education," a thin piece of sanded pine wood, 18 inches long, with ten times the zap of the flyswatter. I hated it. I recall only one of the five board member names printed on the paddle: Rosy Butts.

Rosy was one mean lady. Especially when she showed up immediately after an offense. If Dad delayed the inevitable correction, though, Rosy tended to be less cruel. I had mixed feelings about the two alternatives. Did I want to get the punishment over with, knowing it may be harsher? Or did I want to prolong the agony and wait for a kinder and gentler enforcer? I found both scenarios to be deficient.

Sometimes Rosy was not available. If we happened to be in the great outdoors with low-hanging branches handy, Dad would instruct me to use my knife to cut my own switch. This was a tough crash course in decision-making skills. I certainly didn't want one with too much smart. But if I came back with one that was too wimpy, Dad might cut his own.

Luckily, I didn't get enough licks to perfect switch cutting.

~ ~ ~

THEN THERE WAS THE BELT. Although it rarely saw the light of day, it did see a full moon a time or two.

One day Kenny and I were lazily riding our bikes, chewing on Sugar Daddies we had just purchased down at Elliott's Grocery. I was already feeling the sugar buzz. We passed Mrs. Wilson sitting on her porch. We smiled and waved. She returned the wave, but then offered an unwanted warning. She told us we needed to watch all the candy eating or we'd get worms.

My first thought was that I already had them and they had a voracious appetite for sweets. How differently my day would have gone if I'd kiddingly shared this thought with Mrs. Wilson. However, an ornery streak rose up in me, and I yelled at her, "You're not my mother!"

She responded with something that sounded like, "We'll see about that."

I gritted my teeth, and both my upper and lower incisors cemented themselves to the confection. That was probably a good thing because it kept me from getting in any deeper. It always amazed me how quickly my mouth could mess up a perfect day. As Kenny and I rode toward the school playground, I already regretted talking to our youth leader like that.

I would regret it a lot more when I got home that afternoon. Dad was waiting on the porch for me, and from his stony expression, I knew right away I was in trouble. I ran quickly down the list of the day's possible infractions he might have gotten wind of. I was pretty sure it would be the one involving who my mother was.

Sure enough, he asked me what I had said to Mrs. Wilson. I repeated those four words, not nearly as cocky as I had been that morning. In fact, there was an unmistakable whimper in my voice.

I knew I had blown it. First of all, in Tippecanoe she *was* my mother. All the ladies were our "mothers." We expected to get a talking to from them occasionally, and they would say all the same stuff our own mothers would say.

Second, and even worse, I had disrespected an authority figure. I was sure even my worms were cowering in shame.

The belt must have hurt Dad something awful if, like he said, it hurt him worse than it hurt me. He said he did it for my own good and because he loved me. Love sure can sting sometimes.

~ ~ ~

THE BELT MADE one other unforgettable appearance.

Dad had poured a new slab of concrete right outside the back door. Mom was the most excited about it since the old cracked and uneven one had tripped her twice. It was especially perilous when she was on the attack with the swatter. The new slab was not only safer, but it looked great. Dad took time to admire his work before cleaning up his tools. Then, just for show, he pressed a coin into the center of it—an irresistible, shiny 50-cent piece.

Dad had preached recently about the powerful love of money. It was true. I did love that coin. Enough to pull it out an hour later, before the cement had a permanent hold on it. I hid it in my room. Immediately, a knot started to develop in my stomach. Did I actually think Dad wouldn't find out?

Fifteen minutes later, Dad discovered the vandalism and called a meeting. He got right to the point. He told us we would all get a spanking if someone didn't confess. We all—even the guilty party—eyed each other suspiciously. We knew it couldn't be our new brother Dave. Only six months old and confined to his playpen, he hadn't yet cultivated a love of filthy mammon. Paula had never been a thief. Seven-year-old Lloyd was the likely suspect.

My mind was already doing its shifty work in transferring the guilt to my sibling. Sometimes I would try to alter just about any reality to save my skin.

After three minutes of overwhelming tension, though, a confession was made. I was more shocked than anyone else in the room . . . because it wasn't me! Paula, to restore the peace, had stepped up. Dad asked for the coin, but she said she'd already lost it.

For several ugly seconds, I considered letting my sister be a martyr. But my mind had already traveled back to a strangely similar situation. I was six and Paula was four. Dad had discovered that somebody had torn a page out of one of his books. He issued the dreaded ultimatum that all his offspring would be punished if no one confessed. To keep the peace, Paula took the blame—and got the punishment. But there was no peace for me. Even at six, I well understood gross injustice.

Now, still only a pre-teen, I had circumnavigated one of those circles of life, and I was being given another chance. I could do better, or I could blow it again. Would I try to protect my reputation, already rather shoddy, or would I add a building block to my fledgling character?

This was one time in my life I chose to build. I confessed. When I did, Paula shot me a stunned look. I was sure she now knew I was the page-tearing culprit at the beginning of this circle. She didn't get a spanking for lying, but Mom and she had a long talk afterwards about when it was appropriate to confess.

I *did* get a spanking. And it was redemptive for me. Even though I never fessed up to the prior offense, I felt relieved after the meeting with the belt. I had paid for those wrong choices, and now they were behind me. Corporal punishment, administered in love, did me no harm. Rather, it instilled in me a strong respect for authority to this day.

And there was a side benefit from these two experiences. It didn't come from Dad or Mom, but from my sister. Paula gave me a peek into the love Jesus has for me. He was willing to take my punishment in order to restore the peace within me. Thankfully, His gift didn't require a redemptive spanking. Just my willingness to embrace it.

Chapter 11

Mushroom Soup, Fruitcake, and an Eleven-Year Pizza Fast

I STOICALLY ENDURED bike wrecks, bone fractures, and lacerations. A dentist's drill or doctor's needle, however, could set off a weepy, wimpy reaction in me. And even stronger tearful emotions might accompany humiliation at the hands of my peers or shame at disappointing my parents. But the strangest triggers to opening my tear ducts were encounters with food.

My first emotional food experience came when I was seven. We still lived in northern Ohio and Dad worked at a nearby factory. Every day, he went to work with his lunchbox containing a sandwich and a thermos of soup. One day, he brought home some unfinished lunch. He poured his leftover chicken noodle soup into the shiny silver cup that screwed onto the top of his thermos and offered it to me. It was so tasty that the next day I asked him to hit me again.

He handed me the silver cup. As soon as I smelled it, I reconsidered. Wrinkling my nose, I asked what it was.

"Mushroom soup. It's good. Try it," he replied.

I gagged over a sip. *That's a matter of opinion.*

"Mom can have it," I said, suddenly feeling generous.

"You asked for it. You'll eat it and you'll like it," Dad said matter-of-factly. "Kids in China would be glad to have a bowl of that."

Maybe . . . until they smelled it.

I tried again. My throat rejected it, violently returning it to the cup. My eyes filled with tears, sympathetic to the trauma my tongue was experiencing.

"Go ahead and keep spitting it out, but you'll stay right there until it's all gone," Dad said calmly.

I didn't understand why I had to eat something that my taste buds had clearly identified as toxic. Maybe Dad thought he was building my character. All I could see it was doing was turning me into a crybaby.

Dad softened a bit at my tears until Mom said, "It won't hurt him."

What? Mom was usually on my side, but not in this forced feeding. Knowing I couldn't win against the tag team, I picked up the cup and chugged down the lumpy gray slop. Then I raced off to rinse the worse-than-nasty taste out of my mouth.

I didn't cry any more about food until Christmas that same year.

~ ~ ~

WE ALWAYS ATE CHRISTMAS DINNER at Grandma and Grandpa's house. At that time, we lived less than a quarter mile from them, so we had plenty of time Christmas morning to tear open our presents, empty our stockings, and play with our new treasures at home before heading down the road to eat our big holiday meal. By mid-afternoon, all the relatives had arrived, including Dad's brother and sister and their families. That year, most of us crowded into the living room where Grandpa had his projector set up.

I had worked up a man-sized appetite from all the morning's excitement. A smell drifted in from the kitchen that overpowered even the strong aromas of ham, potatoes, and pumpkin pie. Grandma appeared in the doorway and asked if anyone wanted a fruitcake appetizer.

For years I had heard good things about fruitcake from my grandparents. I raced into the kitchen and pulled a chair up to the table. Paula joined me. Everyone else remained in the living room to watch Grandpa's slide show.

Grandma removed the warm concoction from the oven and placed it on the table in front of us. Close up it smelled a little funny, and it didn't look all that appetizing, but what could be bad about fruit and cake—two of my favorite foods? I was almost drooling by the time I shoveled in my first bite.

It took only a chew or two for me to conclude that, whatever this was, it should *not* be called "cake." Mom's cakes were fluffy and moist. This was as dense and dry as a dehydrated sponge. The fruit pieces were like leather. The overall taste was sickeningly sweet. No wonder everybody except Paula and me chose to watch Grandpa's vacation slides instead of partake in the *non*-appetizer course.

Those food tears welled up in my eyes again. I couldn't swallow. I didn't want to hurt Grandma's feelings, though, so I kept loading chunks into my mouth. Fortunately, Grandma wasn't watching closely; I probably looked like a hamster with his cheek pouches stuffed with seeds. As soon as I cleaned my plate, I headed straight for the bathroom to spit it all into the toilet.

If Paula didn't like the fruitcake, she never showed it. However, she excused herself from the table as soon as I exited the bathroom. No doubt, Grandma had her suspicions of what we were up to, but she never said a word about it.

I couldn't believe how incredible everything tasted when we all sat down to eat later. Even the Brussels sprouts!

~ ~ ~

MRS. MARTIN was good friends with Mom, and she often came to the house to visit. Since I saw so much of her at school, I usually played outside while she was there. One day, Mom called me inside. Mrs. Martin had brought a homemade pizza. As soon as I saw it, I made a face.

In all my eleven years, I had never tried pizza. Not that I didn't have numerous opportunities. Every so often, Mom would make this strange round food from a box kit. It never looked appetizing to me. Maybe it had something to do with the mushrooms she liked to add to the toppings.

No one ever minded that I didn't eat any since that meant more for them. They didn't care that I made a bologna sandwich instead. Dad even sliced my bologna for me and patted me on the head. I couldn't believe Dad and Mom never made me eat the pizza. What happened to the rule in stone that we had to eat what was put on the table? I felt like a big shot. I got away with something every time pizza was on the menu at home.

Mrs. Martin had brought pizza to school once. All the other kids gobbled up their slices as if they hadn't eaten in a week. I was hungry, but not that hungry. I was relieved that Mrs. Martin didn't make me eat any.

But in my house that day, she said, "Butch, will you try just one bite of this pizza I made for you and your family? Please do it for me."

Yikes! I didn't want to disappoint her. I stared at her handiwork as thoughts swirled in my mind.

Why did she have to ask me to taste it? And in front of Mom. If Mom wasn't here, I could decline, though it would involve a lie, like I'll break out in hives if I eat it. I don't see any mushrooms . . . but they could be hiding under all that cheese. She did say "just one bite." Maybe I can pretend to chew that little bit and keep it in my mouth till I can excuse myself.

I picked up a slice, held my nose, and bit off the cheesy point decorated with a sausage crumble. As I fake-chewed, my taste buds experienced something new and wondrous. The crust was chewy but slightly crispy. The moist sausage tasted like Saturday morning breakfast. The tomato sauce had spices I wasn't familiar with, but I wanted to know them better. And I love cheese. In fact, I love tomato soup with grilled cheese sandwiches, and this was *twice* as good. The flavor combination exploding in my mouth would rival even Miss Gilbody's peanut butter cookies. And that is saying a lot.

What happened next was totally unexpected, and totally embarrassing. Tears shot out of my eyes right there in front of my teacher. I was thinking about all the times I had turned pizza down, all the bologna sandwiches I had eaten (that Dad so graciously assisted with) while my family was enjoying this food of the gods, and all the good eating I had missed for so many years.

Luckily for me, Lloyd and Paula weren't there when I cried. The only ones to tell on me were Mom and Mrs. Martin. Mom wouldn't want her friends to know her oldest son was a crybaby, and Mrs. Martin would never betray my humiliation. So I was safe on that account—until now.

~ ~ ~

I WILL EAT almost anything now. Even a bite or two of fruitcake . . . if it is the only thing in the house . . . and if I haven't eaten anything in at least three days. I will eat a casserole with mushroom soup in it as long as the fungi remain anonymous. But Bonnie hasn't been able to get me to eat sardines or chicken livers yet. She hasn't tried real hard though. She hates to see a grown man cry.

Chapter 12

Bulk Purchases
and a Disappointed Haydn

WHEN DAD LEFT HIS SAWMILL BUSINESS to go into the ministry, his salary dropped from $30,000 to $3,000. I didn't even realize that we had become poor because we always had everything we needed. My parents were pros at squeezing the most copper out of every penny.

They were always finding ways to stretch the lean budget. They frequented the day old bakery and bought food in quantity when it was on sale at the market. Sometimes our freezer was full of gallon jugs of milk. Mom canned the produce that parishioners generously shared with their pastor. She often sewed Paula's dresses.

Before Costco and Sam's Club came on the scene, Dad and Mom had already bought into bulk purchasing. Only, Dad had to make his own package deals. When our coats wore out, we made a trip to the store in Uhrichsville where Dad would dicker with the manager until he got an acceptable price on buying a round of new coats.

One time a traveling salesman came through town. When he left, all the Spencer kids were shod with the same kind of shoes. They were some type of plastic made to look like leather, and they stunk after two days. We still had to wear them.

Dr. Trimnell was not excluded from Dad's bulk buying mania. If one of us got sick, we all had to pay him a visit. A shot for one meant a shot for all. It must have been preventative and, therefore, cheaper in the long run.

One of the biggest expenses was eyeglasses. Paula brought a note home from school one day. Her teacher wrote that she had observed Paula squinting at the board. Soon after that, Dad took all three of us out of school to go see the eye doctor in New Philadelphia. Nine-month-old Dave stayed home with Mom, safe from the possibility of being called Frog-eyes any time soon.

We all failed our vision tests so Dad ordered three pairs of glasses. It was buy two, get one free for the minister. I'm sure that even if only one of us had needed glasses that day, though, he still would have gotten the other two pairs and held them in reserve.

We picked them up two weeks later. The following morning, three Spencer kids sat around the breakfast table munching Shredded Wheat and wearing shiny new plastic frames. Now we were *all* squinting, trying to get used to the strange new fixtures on our faces.

I dreaded the debut of my new spectacles at school. That morning I took a detour on my bike, looking for a prospective place to have an accident. I would, of course, land on my face and—oh, horrors!—break my glasses. I pushed my bike up Henry's hill and took the sledding bank on the ride down. As I neared the launching point, I realized it wasn't in me to wreck on purpose, no matter how much I despised my new spectacles. I sailed over the bank and had no problem staying upright, even as I double-bounced my landing. Oh well, there was always recess.

I pulled my bike into school five minutes from being tardy. Immediately, as if they had been waiting on my arrival, two seventh graders hurled names at me. "Hey, Coke Bottle!" "Look at Four-eyes." A moment of anger quickly turned into humiliation, and I burst into tears. I didn't have time to sulk though. I jerked off my glasses and stuffed them in my pocket. Then I dried my eyes and walked into class.

Mrs. Martin greeted me, then went about her morning rituals. I wondered why she hadn't said anything more. Surely she could see I was struggling to hide tears. And she knew I was supposed to be wearing glasses. Dad and Mom would have told her.

Everything else that morning was normal until science class. The lesson, by some odd quirk, was about the human eye. Funny. I thought we were studying algae.

We learned about the functions of the parts of the eye and some ocular diseases. Then Mrs. Martin explained her own vision problems. As a child, she needed glasses and was shy about wearing them at first, but their usefulness in helping her to see the board in school far outweighed her embarrassment.

Before sending us out for recess, Mrs. Martin asked Bruce if anyone had ever teased him about his glasses. Wow! I had forgotten Bruce even wore glasses. He said someone had once called him Window Face, but he just ignored them. If tall, athletic Bruce could wear glasses, so could I. And if they were good for Mrs. Martin, then they were good for me.

Now I was ready for recess—my first recess wearing glasses. I had some seventh graders to ignore.

~ ~ ~

DAD AND MOM wanted at least one of their children to play piano in church, so they signed all three of us up to take lessons from Mrs. Kelly. I suspected they got a special deal for enrolling all of us at once.

Mrs. Kelly lived in a neighboring town and drove thirteen miles into Tippecanoe once a week to spend an hour and a half with three Spencer children. She gave each of us a half-hour lesson on the piano in the church basement, beginning with Lloyd and ending with me. We had to work all other Saturday activities around our music lessons. To say I wasn't highly motivated was an understatement.

After three months, Mrs. Kelly introduced me to one of her favorite songs: "Papa Haydn's Dead and Gone." The music was from the theme of Haydn's *Surprise Symphony* and sounded similar to the tune of "Twinkle, Twinkle, Little Star."

Papa Haydn's dead and gone
But his memory lingers on,
When his mood was one of bliss
He wrote jolly tunes like this.

Though it had simple notes for the right hand, it required my left hand to accompany with chords. This would be my first real two-handed song as my previous left-hand experience was limited to only my pointer finger pounding away on "Chopsticks."

I was familiar with all the notes in the bass clef. Mrs. Kelly had given me a way to remember them. The spaces were "All Cars Eat Gas" (A-C-E-G), and "Good Boys Do Fine Always" (G-B-D-F-A) was the memory device for the lines of the staff. The latter trick may have helped me read the notes, but in a week I would demonstrate that the statement should not be taken literally.

I had practiced the treble clef every day and had the melody down pat, but I had put off working on the accompaniment. There were only a handful of chords, but my left hand had not been a willing team player. This little star would not twinkle at his lesson. No more blissful mood for Haydn. I expected tears would fall from my teacher's eyes in sadness for Papa.

Before Mrs. Kelly arrived that Saturday, I rode out to Johnny Appleseed's place. I needed a good belt of his spring water to get me through this one. After a long stiff drink, I felt power surge through my veins. I could do this. Suddenly, out of left field, came a new idea, and I found myself riding down the road toward West Chester—the opposite direction from my piano lesson. What I had thought was newfound courage turned out to be flat-out cowardice. I had become "A Wicked Ornery Loser" (A-W-O-L).

At five minutes past two, I was at the house of Mrs. Brown, a member of our church. I had missed my classical music debut. Tears flowed as I told her my predicament. By the time I could get back to the church, my lesson time would be over. At her urging, I called home and explained where I was.

Mom asked me why I had run off. I said it was because I hadn't practiced with my left hand and I didn't want to disappoint Mrs. Kelly or her and Dad, not to mention Mr. Haydn. She told me to ride home and we would talk about it some more.

On the way, I swung by Johnny's oak barrel to grab another few swigs of water. Probably not the smartest idea seeing as how that water seemed to interfere with my compass. This time I made it home though. And I was glad to see Mrs. Kelly had gone.

Dad was pretty mellow on Saturday afternoons. He wanted to conserve his energy for preaching four Sunday sermons, which included the evening service in the Tipp church. So it was Mom who handled this situation. And without the fly swatter.

Mom was Mrs. Martin, Henry, Mrs. Wilson, and King Solomon all rolled into one. She asked why I hadn't come to her and Dad with my problem instead of running off and making it worse. If I had come to them, they might have asked Mrs. Kelly to skip my lesson that week while I worked on my bass clef.

My parents didn't mind me missing one lesson. After all, they were getting a good deal. And they could see the improvement I was making. They figured I had learned my lesson about dodging responsibility. And I had. Still, it wasn't pleasant when I had to call Mrs. Kelly to apologize and tell her I would have my song ready by the next week.

Though I had missed my music session, I learned another important lesson that day: "Butch Accepts Swell Second Chance—Love Erases Failings" (B-A-S-S C-L-E-F).

~ ~ ~

EVERYONE AT SCHOOL got over my glasses after a couple of days, so I did too. And the piano lessons accomplished what my parents hoped. I was the one who ended up playing in church on Sunday evenings when the regular pianist was sick. I could manage the simple hymns Dad chose. But there were always a few requests from the congregation. I had to remind them to stick to songs with no more than three flats or two sharps. Hey, what did they expect from discount piano lessons? Certainly not a young Haydn.

Chapter 13

Backseat Bumper Kids

DAD LOVED SPEED. He drove in dirt track races in Ashtabula, many times on a figure-8 track. Other drivers soon learned of Dad's reluctance to yield, which won him the right-of-way nine times out of ten at the intersection. Once in a while he met up with someone as stubborn as he was and experienced a crash with the ensuing repairs.

In the spring of 1958, Dad and his brother-in-law each came home the same day with a new car, both sporty '58 models. Before their engines even had a chance to cool, they were racing down Footville-Richmond Road in Dorset. Their course was as straight as a runway, and they flew side by side through the flat farmland. At that time of year, they could see forever and would be forewarned of any other vehicles on the road. It's a good thing they weren't on a figure-8 because likely neither of them would have yielded to the other. Both cars returned in one piece, though I would hesitate to describe the motors and drive trains as new after that.

Maybe Dad had a close call out there among the winter wheat for it was soon after that race he yielded to the Lord. When he was baptized, though, his right foot must have shot up out of the water, escaping some of the sanctifying effect. That less purified extremity sure came in handy in his first charge in Tippecanoe when he had to commute between his three churches every Sunday morning.

When our family went anywhere together in the car, we older kids would space ourselves out on the back seat like birds on a telephone wire while Mom held Dave on her lap in the front. This was before seat belt and car seat requirements had come along.

Dad was a good driver, always in control so as not to endanger others on the road, but he wasted no time getting from point A to point B. Sometimes he would top a hill while pushing the speed limit. It would lift all the lightweights off of the seat and "tickle our bellies." It always brought a "Jim!" from Mom, but all of us in the back seat would beg for more. The roller coaster sensation happened only when we weren't expecting it, which is probably why it was so much fun.

Sometimes it was a challenge to maintain our own sacred territory. Dad had covered the back seat with a thick, glossy protector. He might have even waxed it; he liked his cars to be shiny inside and out. When he encountered a sharp turn, it was like bumper cars without the cars: brother into sister into brother into door. Dad would have an impish look in his eyes as he watched us in the rearview mirror, arguing with each other and brushing off the cooties.

"You touched me!"

"Stay in your own spot!"

"Take your cooties back!"

We had better not argue too much or Dad's expression would turn to annoyance and his long arm would reach back and flail the air. It didn't matter to him if he got the instigator, or even the most vocal backseat occupant. He would settle for the slowest one. It was actually great fun unless he grabbed me. Then I might get a pinch or a nasty squeeze.

The shelf under the back window, common in sedans of that time, was good for something other than bobble-head dogs and spare ball caps. Sometimes Lloyd tired of the bickering and climbed up there for a breather. That allowed Paula and me to hug our respective doors and enlarge the area the cooties had to travel from one host to the other. That is, if they could even navigate the slippery surface.

Too much arguing could also get one of us moved up front between Dad and Mom. That brought mixed feelings for me. I'd get away from my siblings and their insect—or is it arachnid?—friends, but I'd better be prepared for two arms to wallop me in the face if Dad had to stop fast. Mom usually had quicker reactions, which I counted on since mom arms are softer.

Once when I was riding up front, Dad braked hard for a cow. Dad and Mom were both too slow and I was walloped instead by the dash. My forehead stayed black and blue for days. Dad must have been speeding. I could tell he felt guilty. Until my normal color returned, his right foot acted almost as sanctified as his left one.

~ ~ ~

BEFORE DAWN ON THANKSGIVING DAY, the family piled into our Ford and headed north to Grandma and Grandpa Spencer's to spend the day with relatives on Dad's side of the family. Dad was driving noticeably slower, even though my bruises were long gone. In honor of the holiday, we in the back seat observed an unofficial moratorium on arguing for the first hour. Eventually, we got around to our bickering. Because we were still drowsy, we had to work at it. But work at it we did because it's a kid's duty to do so.

After half an hour of our fussing, Dad said, "Don't make me stop this car." We'd heard that plenty of times, but it usually took a lot longer than 30 minutes to warrant that statement. And usually when he made that declaration, it was only a threat. Occasionally, though, he followed through. It had been a long time since the last pullover. That time it hadn't ended well.

Perhaps remembering that incident, we quieted down and just made faces at each other. I could see Dad's eyes in the rearview mirror monitoring the goings-on, but I couldn't tell if he was mad or not. Lloyd got bored and climbed up in the back window; Paula and I took our normal positions glued to the doors.

After a short nap, Lloyd was ready for a little action. He poked Paula. She thought I did it. Hostilities flared up between my sister and me while Lloyd went back to "sleep." As I loudly pleaded my innocence to Paula, we heard the sound we hated: the crunch of tires on gravel along the shoulder of the road. Lloyd descended from his perch, and we started making up in the back even before the wheels stopped rolling. Not only close siblings, but best friends forever.

Mom turned around and said, "You kids should have listened to your father." As always, though, she was ready to come to our defense if needed.

Three unblinking statues sat in the back seat holding their collective breath. Dad turned 180 degrees and looked into each of our faces. He asked if he could say something. *Asked?* Right then I knew we were in unfamiliar territory.

Dad was not angry. In fact, his eyes were moist and held a soft expression. Our jaws dropped like rocks. This was not a side of Dad we often saw.

"I am thankful for each and every one of you in this car. I know I don't tell you that enough. Some day you guys will be thankful for each other." He told us to stand, and he put his right arm around all three of us. Then his left arm encircled Mom and Dave, and he pulled us all into a big family hug.

The back seat was uncommonly quiet for the last few miles. I can't speak for Lloyd or Paula, but I was busy savoring the best backseat squeeze I ever got.

Chapter 14

Cold Weather and Warm Teasing

WE HAD SOME MIGHTY COLD WINTERS in the early '60s. How cold were they? They were so cold I have to wear gloves just writing about them. You might need to let this chapter thaw a little before you read it.

The coldest day I remember was 27 below. It was a Friday. I had to scrape ice off the inside of the parsonage window to read the huge metal thermometer hanging outside. Snow had fallen throughout the week and built up several inches on the ground. We rarely got a snow day, so I was excited beyond measure when Mrs. Martin called early that morning to say there would be no school. It wasn't canceled because the school would be too cold —the school furnace did a sufficient job—but because both buses refused to start.

I probably should have stayed indoors and just watched the snow on the TV screen, but the bitter temperature provided a challenge I couldn't ignore. I offered to ride my bike to the post office and get the mail for Dad. Bundled up like the Michelin

Man, I donned Dad's old sawmill goggles and headed out. No degree of cold would stop this mail run.

The brilliant sunlight mined gems from the snow and displayed them against a dazzling blue backdrop. My tires rode low from the reduced air pressure. They crunched loudly and crisply that day on the snow-covered road. I heard a car engine cranking in the distance. Someone was splitting wood. A door opened and then closed with a thud. The slightest sound carried in the crystal clear air.

I had one of Mom's long scarves wrapped around my face. It was toasty, but it caused fog and ice to form on the goggles. I finally took the scarf off so I could see to keep my bike on the road. The moving air felt like thousands of tiny needles using my face as a pincushion.

After the quarter-mile ride, I dropped my bike on the sidewalk and hurried up to the post office door. Nothing happened when I turned the knob. No way it could be locked. I couldn't imagine the postmaster not showing up. After all, he worked for the USPS and adhered to their all-encompassing, even if unofficial, motto. I pounded on the door. Sure enough, Mr. Carson was there, but had forgotten to unlock it.

Mr. Carson said strange things to me every time he saw me.

"Why do you have so many coats on? Do you think it's winter?"

"With your red nose maybe I should call you Rudolph."

"Oh. Your mail? Now, let's see, is your name Wiener Schnitzel or Whatcha Macallit?"

Even if his comments were silly, he delivered them in such a serious tone I never knew how to take them—or him. I didn't know him well. He didn't attend our church, so our family didn't have much occasion to socialize with him. I couldn't tell if he was making fun of me, so I always felt a tad uneasy.

On this particular day he greeted me with, "What did you come for? A huckleberry pie? Oh, you're looking for mail? Sorry. No mail today. How about a cup of angleworms?"

I didn't know how to react. I began to sweat, whether from Mr. Carson's weirdness or my excessive clothing, I wasn't sure. I quickly thanked him and returned to the icebox.

There wasn't a bit of breeze. As I passed the hardware store on my return ride, I saw wood smoke rising straight up from the chimney. Inside, a few old guys would be gathered around the huge potbelly stove in the middle of the floor. They would be sipping coffee poured from a large metal pot that had a permanent home on the stove's flat surface. Their conversation would be about the good old days, and how the kids today just had it too easy.

When I got home, I peeled myself like an onion till I got down to the last layer. I left my clothes piled on the bedroom floor, knowing I would layer back up to go outside later.

I found Mom in the kitchen fixing lunch and sat down to watch her.

"Something on your mind, Butch?"

"I just rode to the post office to see if there was any mail." I didn't offer any more.

Finally Mom said, "And . . .?

"There wasn't any."

"And . . .?

"Well . . . Mr. Carson always says crazy things to me." I told her some of his strange statements. "I don't know why he does that."

"He's teasing you," she said.

"Why?"

"It's his way of having fun with you. Maybe he's trying to get to know you better. He's saying he likes you."

After Mom told me that, being teased didn't seem quite as bad. In fact, I almost hoped Mr. Carson *would* say something weird the next time I went for the mail.

~ ~ ~

AFTER LUNCH, Lloyd, Paula, and I went across the road to skate. Stillwater Creek had overrun its banks again late in the year, and now the overflow had frozen solid, creating our own icy wonderland. By this time, the mercury had stretched all the way up to zero.

I found Eddie, Jerry, and Kenny near the huge fire that someone had built in the center of the temporary rink. It was always amazing to me that the ice underneath did not melt. Skaters were rhythmically circling the fire. Among them were a few couples who went to the high school in Freeport. The cold gave them a perfect excuse to skate close. It was our job as little punks to give them a hard time. We yelled annoying things as they skated around the circle, but with little effect. We might as well have been invisible.

I was careful to not direct any of my pestering at Tim Wilson and his girl, even if I wasn't being noticed. Tim took me cruising in his '41 Ford hot rod. That thing could move! Dad and Mom let me ride with him because he was the youth group leader's son. He also sang specials in our church and neighboring churches, so he was all right in their book. I wasn't about to do anything to get him mad at me and jeopardize my joyriding privileges.

Tired of not being able to raise any reactions from the high schoolers, I studied the fire. It had burned low. Maybe I could get a good run and jump over it. Spotting a pile of coats lying on the other side of the fire where skaters had discarded their top layers, I decided to do a practice jump first.

I started back about fifty feet and skated as fast as I could, arms pumping. Five feet from the coats, I left the ice, legs running in the air. I came down soft—though considerably less than graceful. I had landed on the far edge of the coats, fallen backwards, and sailed across the ice on my back on a green plaid skimmer. Hearing the crowd's applause, I realized I was no longer invisible. I could feel my already cold-reddened face burn brighter. Fire jumping would not be added to my résumé any time soon.

Lloyd was getting some attention of his own. At seven years old, he could glide in and out of the other skaters, and even switch to skating backwards. All the girls noticed him. He seemed to enjoy it. I studied him, trying to figure out what made him so attractive to the females. Somehow he had picked up the name Peaches from them. Maybe it was from his rosy cheeks.

Bitterly cold feet finally transported my siblings and me back home. The older kids would keep the fire blazing and hang around the ice for several more hours. Our family had plans of their own for the evening. We would celebrate this snow day to the max.

~ ~ ~

AFTER WE THAWED OUT and had a bite to eat, Mom and we kids walked to the Longs' house. It was only a tenth of a mile down the dead-end road past Henry's. We visited there often since Kenny's mother Marge had quickly become one of Mom's best friends. Dad and Dave didn't go with us on this night. Dad would spend the time working on his Sunday sermon.

The Long family was about as rugged as they come. Mr. Long rode his moped thirteen miles each way to work over in Uhrichsville every workday, including this frigid day. That took away any bragging rights I thought I had about riding my bike to the post office. Mr. Long trapped in any weather and cleaned raccoon pelts in his unheated basement all winter. The rest of the family, including Kenny's younger brother and sister, were just as tough. On cold days like this, the woodstove burned hot. That was their sole source of heat.

The Longs had no TV, but we listened to the radio at their house. The favorite of all the kids was *Gunsmoke*. We made up for the lack of video by chasing each other around the room with guns and lassos. Our moms would listen to programs like the *Bing Crosby-Rosemary Clooney Show* and *Yours Truly, Johnny Dollar*. While they listened, we would play hide and seek, tag, or less physical games like Snakes and Ladders or Skunk.

Soon after we arrived at the Longs' that evening, all of us kids rushed outside. Though it was almost dark, the snow reflected the starlight, illuminating the backyard well enough for what we had in mind: war. We chose sides and each one started to build a fort. The powdery snow would not cooperate, however, so we called a truce.

The four oldest kids then grabbed buckets and carried snow to create one huge mountain as high as the tallest of us. Then we ran down the hill and dived into it. We didn't take turns; we just hoped no one was in the spot where we landed. It was fifteen minutes of euphoric chaos. Then we stiffly returned to the house, our sweaty layers having frozen into armor.

I didn't know how cold I was until I sat huddled with the others around the woodstove. My fingers and toes stung as feeling crept back into them. But I soon forgot the pain as the smell of popcorn and chocolate cake wafted from the kitchen. We washed the treats down with cherry Fizzies. And on this special snow day and Friday night combination, it was all we could eat and drink.

After we stuffed ourselves, we played cowboys and Indians for a while. Since it was almost as cold inside the house as outside, the activity helped to warm us. At some point, we couldn't keep our eyes open any longer. Mom walked back home but left her brood there for the night. We went to bed with no complaints.

All six of us slept in the same bed upstairs. The temperature was dropping and not much warm air was rising. The woodstove just wasn't cutting it, so we had half a dozen quilts piled on top of us.

I should have laid off the all-you-can-drink Fizzies. About midnight the urge to go hit hard. A metal pot sat in the corner of the bedroom behind a curtain, but I wasn't about to use it. The alternative was the outhouse up the hill in the backyard. The snow light was still on the job. I ran all the way. When I returned and squeezed myself back under the quilts, my freezing feet brushed someone and they screamed. No one fully awakened, though, and I buried my head till morning.

~ ~ ~

IN THE MORNING, Mrs. Long fed us an early breakfast of eggs and bacon. Then she made Paula, Lloyd, and me bundle up before walking back home since it was below zero.

We stayed inside all morning and watched TV. The last good show, *Sky King*, was on at noon. By the time it was over, the thermometer had risen to 7 degrees. I bundled back up to make a run to the post office. This time I left Mom's scarf and Dad's goggles behind.

Mr. Carson was busy closing up and didn't say too much when I came in. He continued working with his back to me. I would just have to cast the first line.

"Hey, Mr. Carson, I'll take you up on the angleworms you offered me yesterday. I'll wait right here while you go out back and dig 'em up."

Boy, did I get him good.

"Well, Butch, that's not the way you do it," he said in his slow, serious voice. "When I get home, I'll plant some worm seeds. There should be a big cup of juicy worms come about April."

He turned halfway around and gave me a sideways glance. I detected the slightest wrinkle under the one eye I could see.

Good one, Mr. Carson.

This teasing stuff wasn't bad, not bad at all.

Chapter 15

Matchmaking Tippecanoe Style

2 in a car
2 little kisses
2 weeks later
Mr. and Mrs. (Butch and Sarah)

AN ENTRY from my sixth-grade autograph book revealed that the possibility of a romance with Sarah did not come entirely from my imagination. Every other page had a poem about the two of us. We seemed to be an item with many of our classmates. Not with Jerry, however. Until the day Sarah and I would have our two little kisses and become Mr. and Mrs., I would have competition. And then there was Sarah herself who seemed to be in the dark.

It wasn't just my classmates trying to get Sarah and me together. The adults got into the act as well. An older lady from one of Dad's other churches signed my book.

When you get married
And live by a lake,
Please send me a piece
Of your wedding cake.

This was good stuff. She probably wrote the same thing in every book, but at the time, I was sure she had written it specially for Sarah and me. I wanted Sarah to read it, along with the other entries. Maybe she would see that we were meant to be together. Did she like two-week engagements? Living by the lake? Clendening was conveniently close by.

Fearful of tripping over my tongue, I asked Paula to get Sarah to sign my book. She added a poem written in her cryptic style.

Friends are like diamonds
Precious but rare,
False ones like autumn leaves
Found everywhere.

Apparently, Cupid had run out of arrows. I analyzed this entry a thousand times, but I found nothing to give me even a glimmer of hope. First of all, I was aiming to be more than just a friend. But if that's all I was in Sarah's eyes, was I a rare, sparkling diamond . . . or an autumn leaf waiting its turn to be raked into a pile and burned?

~ ~ ~

THE ADULTS IN TIPPECANOE innocently encouraged romances among the young people. They didn't worry about things getting out of hand. They knew that we knew that two little kisses could lead to a quick shotgun wedding. It was written in our autograph books.

For Sarah and me, it was our parents who had begun the matchmaking as soon as my family moved to Tippecanoe. I had seen Sarah at church on our first Sunday, and I was taken with her shoulder-length black hair and nice smile, but we hadn't talked. By a stroke of luck, her father was the head of the pastor welcoming committee. He and Dad had hit it off right away. Before we even had all our boxes unpacked, Mr. Parker invited our family to his farm for a barbecue.

It was my first time on a farm. I was still getting acquainted with my country surroundings when Sarah appeared. She seemed to be watching me, so I had to do something entertaining to keep her attention—and quickly. I scanned the yard and noticed some chickens strutting around. Without hesitation, I began to chase a dark red hen in circles.

Dad and Mr. Parker settled into comfortable chairs on the porch of the farmhouse to enjoy glasses of lemonade. They got a kick out of my one-man show. I finally gave up on the chicken and climbed a huge tree nearby, feeling nervous under Sarah's gaze. Our fathers laughed and teased me, saying they thought Sarah and I made a cute couple. I objected vigorously and faked being upset. Dad allowed me to throw a fit when he teased me. I usually got mad for real, but that day I kind of liked it. Sarah was still watching me.

Our moms were busy doing the grilling, so they didn't see the show I put on for Sarah. Later that day, though, our fathers would pass the matchmaking ball to their wives. It was a comfort to have our parents in my court . . . even if it didn't help my game.

~ ~ ~

NOTHING IN A YEAR AND A HALF had brought me into Sarah's sights, including the recent poems and well-wishes in my book. Maybe Mrs. Wilson would open Sarah's eyes to what a great catch I might be. As the youth leader, she was also the Christmas play director. That year she selected me to be Joseph. Sarah would be the missus. Thanks to Mrs. Wilson, Butch and Sarah would not only marry up; they would have a kid besides.

As ideal as this sounded in theory, I had my doubts that the marriage would last till Christmas since Sarah had no romantic leanings toward me. And if she did ever feel inclined to utter a word to me, I would probably faint on the spot. For real.

I was relieved at the first play practice to learn that Mary and Joseph had no dialogue. Not unusual for a married couple. Maybe this could work.

Jerry prayed it wouldn't, but he was less than happy with the answer he got. Mrs. Wilson had picked him to be the angel, and he had to proclaim to Joseph, "Do not be afraid to take Mary home as your wife!" I decided it might be best not to turn my back on him. Angel or not.

There were no chickens to chase or trees to climb, so I would have to come up with other ingenious activities if Sarah happened to look my way. The only animals on the scene were a donkey and a cow, both costumed by Mom. It hadn't taken long for her to learn that the church community had high expectations for the preacher's wife. Any job with no takers found its way to her.

The animals narrated the play and occasionally argued about which of them had the biggest role in the Savior's birth. The donkey had nearly broken his back carrying Mary 100 miles from Nazareth to Bethlehem; the cow was on the verge of starvation from giving up her feeding trough for the baby Jesus.

Jerry's older brothers played the squabblers. Tony donned the cow costume. He was Sarah's age and good-looking. He seemed a logical match for Sarah, but fortunately for me, he had no interest in her. Carl was the donkey. This presented an interesting possibility. As Jerry and I watched Carl hee-hawing uncontrollably at that first practice, we got the same idea.

We would both try to get Carl to put in a free plug for us with Sarah. Since he would take any dare, I would lobby him to blurt out "Butch loves Sarah" sometime during the play. Jerry would sway him toward "Jerry loves Sarah." Whichever he brayed, he would follow it with a loud hee-haw. Parents would roll their eyes and laugh it off; they were used to Carl. And it would be more impressive than sky-writing to Sarah.

The question was which of us would have the greatest clout with the donkey?

~ ~ ~

WHEN CHRISTMAS EVE ARRIVED, the question became moot. Kenny showed up with Jerry's angel costume. *Jerry must be sick*, I thought. *Good. Now he won't be here to influence Carl.*

My countenance dropped, however, as Mrs. Wilson told us that *Carl* had become ill and Jerry had agreed to take his place as the donkey. We wouldn't have any of Carl's crazy shenanigans after all. I decided to just play it straight and be the best husband I could be to Mary. But that would be more difficult than I imagined.

Every chance Jerry got during the play, he would sidle up to Sarah and get her to pet him. Then he would walk past me and "accidentally" step on my toe. After the third toe-crunching, I "accidentally" tripped him. He fell against the manger, bouncing Baby Jesus across the stage. Mary burst into tears. No more affection for the donkey. And a brutal scowl for me.

That was my first prolonged eye contact with Sarah . . . and my last for a long, long time.

Chapter 16

Petrified Gum and
Shoddy Business Practices

BY THE AGE OF ELEVEN, I could no longer live on a fixed income. My allowance of 25 cents a week could get me a Saturday after-noon feast: a 16-ounce pop, a bag of chips, and a monster candy bar (as long as I returned an empty bottle for the two-cent deposit). Or maybe I'd even rush out and buy five packs of ball cards. The other six days of the week, however, would find me with empty pockets.

I received cash from relatives for Christmas and my birthday, but Dad and Mom made me put half of that into savings. And with all the offerings at Woolworth's Five and Dime, the spend-ing money didn't last long. I had to get a job.

I found one at a farm north of town, working with Jerry and his brother Tony. As bales of hay came off the baler, we stacked them on a wagon. For a day's work, we each took a dollar home. My back lasted only a few days. The bales were as big as I was.

I told Dad maybe I should be using a little less back muscle. He told me the church janitor might pay me something to help him. Sure enough, Mr. Cubbage gave me a scraper and told me I'd get a dollar if I removed all the gum from the bottom of the pews. Wow! Though I'd be stealing from the church, I wasn't going to turn down such lucrative work. And my back would get to lie down on the job.

Come Saturday morning, I was flat on the floor of the sanctuary staring up at the profusion of chicle and synthetic rubber stuck under the seats. It hit me why Mr. Cubbage had offered the big money. Some globs were so hardened that they must have christened the pews in 1898. Under the benches my friends regularly occupied was enough gum to hold a tank together. A fair amount was under my seat as well, but that would remain my secret.

I earned my money that day. And I was sure all my friends would appreciate having more space to dispose of their indigestible treats. Word of my scraping job got out, but rather than receiving accolades from my classmates at school on Monday, they heralded me as Gumboy. I liked the money, but I had my pride.

~ ~ ~

I LEFT THE PHYSICAL LABOR BEHIND and focused on coupons and premiums, one being the comics that came in Bazooka bubblegum. Though less enthralled with gum since my pew-scraping experience, I used all my ready cash to buy as much Bazooka gum as I could at Renaker's Market and Elliott's Grocery for a penny a piece.

When my friends found out, they volunteered to help me chew it. That was fine with me. How much gum could one person chew? And besides, it bordered on physical labor. While my crew worked, they passed the comics around to read about the latest happenings of Bazooka Joe and his gang. I supervised carefully to make sure I didn't lose any inventory.

Those Bazooka comics were like money. They could be traded for dozens of different prizes. A magic magnet set comprised of two magnets, two steel balls, a wooden dowel, and instructions for doing magic tricks required 150 comics. I could get a knife with two quality carbon steel blades for 200 comics or a "real camera" that used #127 film for 250.

With some ready cash, I needed way fewer comics for the "valuable prizes." The magnet set required only five comics if I included 30 cents. That would save me $1.15 on buying all that gum, but of course, my buddies would miss the fun of helping me chew it.

I loved my "genuine 22-karat gold-plated ring with your own initial" that adjusted to fit any finger. I got B for Butch as a reminder for Dad, who was calling me Clarence more and more lately.

Another source of coupons was Boyer Mallo Cups and Peanut Butter Smoothie Cups. Each package contained play money in the form of coin cards. The values ranged from five cents to one dollar, but I rarely got the elusive dollar. When I collected 500 points, I could redeem them for ten Mallo Cups. It cost a lot of real money to accumulate 500 points of play money, but it was exciting when the candy arrived in the mail. And the freebies even had coin cards in them to use toward more free candy.

~ ~ ~

MY TRAINER PLANE had made it through the spring without getting shot down, but by the end of the school year, too many hard landings had permanently grounded it. I was itching to fly again, and this time with an upgraded model. But I realized I would have to move past the penny-ante stuff and make some big money. Only a week passed before the answer jumped out at me from the back of a magazine.

"Win Prizes and Gain Business Experience!" the ad promised. Too bad there was no warning that the salesman could become shady in the process. I sent for the catalog and found that for five dollars and the proceeds from selling twenty boxes of greeting cards, I could have my own single engine P-40 Flying Tiger with shark teeth and eyes!

I sold my twenty boxes of cards, paid my $5.00, and received my airplane. The Tiger roared all of three weeks—until I flew it into a fence post and smashed it to smithereens. No amount of bubble gum would ever hold the pieces together. Luckily, I still had my catalog.

When I told Mom I wanted to sell more cards, she wasn't at all happy. She would, once again, have to bug her friends to buy them. And everyone in town was already receiving identical "greeting cards for all occasions" from each other.

I decided my next product would be personalized Christmas cards. They would be pricier at $3.00 a box. I would need to sell 25 boxes to get a Wen Mac P-38 Lightning: a twin-engine bomber with a two-foot wingspan. It would require no money of my own . . . or so the catalog said.

I hoped the townspeople would catch the Christmas spirit early. The adults didn't give the yuletide much thought until after Thanksgiving, but I needed the order postmarked by November 10 to get the printed cards back by the beginning of December.

I started going door-to-door in early October and received blank looks from most of my potential customers. However, with a lot of help from Mom, her Tupperware friends, Dad's flock, the folks from the Assembly of God, and even a Catholic family or two, I made my last needed sale on November 9. Unfortunately, on that same day, I lost the second page of the orders. Not good. It contained printing instructions for the last five customers.

I had to get the order in the mail right away. I could remember the people, but I wasn't sure of all the spellings or exactly how they wanted to personalize. It would have been too embarrassing to go back to my customers. I didn't see the need to tell anyone anyway because I had another blank order sheet. I filled it in the best I could.

I gave Mom all the money I'd collected. She asked to see the order sheets. After glancing over the first one, she handed them both back. I guess she figured the customers knew how they wanted to personalize their cards and she didn't need to check what they wrote. Then she drove me to the post office for a money order. I mailed it and began the wait. I could almost hear those twin engines coming in for a landing.

The next day, page two surfaced. I was horrified to see I had gotten four of the five personalizations wrong. The sound of my P-38 Lightning faded into the wild blue yonder. I knew I should tell someone. I almost did. But I didn't. I shoved it out of my mind the best I could.

A few weeks later, on a Friday afternoon, I picked up my package of Deluxe Personalized Christmas Greeting Cards from Mr. Carson at the post office. When I got home, I quickly opened it and pulled out the orders from page two. I couldn't believe it!

Even the one I got right I got wrong. I spelled Mr. Cubbage's name correctly, but the printer must have misread it. There were twenty cards that read, "Merry Christmas from Chad Cabbage." I had work to do if I was going to make my deliveries the next day.

While my family watched TV that night, I sneaked the cards to the basement. I found my white model airplane paint and worked on Mr. Cubbage's order, covering the misbehaving *a*'s and replacing them with delicately written *u*'s of the same font. The corrected cards were passable, if I didn't look too close. Back in their box they went.

Mom yelled down to see what I was doing. I yelled up that I was painting cards, desperately hoping it sounded like *cars*. Smelling the fumes, she bought my story and went back to watching *Route 66*. Dad had gone over to his study at the church to finish up his sermon on integrity.

I opened the box for the Turners. They had wanted "Sam and Debbie" Turner but they got "Mr. and Mrs." I closed the box and hoped they wouldn't notice. Mr. and Mrs. Franks wanted "and family" on theirs. I obliged on all twenty cards. My good penmanship was coming in handy. On the Martins' cards, I had spelled Harry's name with an *i*. I meticulously changed the *i*'s to *r*'s and painted the dots away. It wasn't going so badly. Maybe I could get a side job with the company correcting their misprints.

The last order presented a bigger challenge: changing *Fillups* to *Phillips*. I needed to hurry. *Father of the Bride* was about half over, and Mom would check on me when it ended. And Dad would return from the church any time. With more paint and my font-matching skill, the names morphed into the correct spelling.

Not a great job, but I completed them before anyone came snooping.

Businessmen sometimes have to make tough decisions, and I had made mine. I went to bed confident that things would work out.

~ ~ ~

IN THE MORNING, the positive feeling had deserted me. Dad, on the other hand, having finished his sermon on honest living, was in a great mood. That was sure to change because he was about to find out that his son was a crook.

It was delivery day, and I couldn't wait any longer to confess my blunder to him. I expected anger and disappointment in return. But no, he seemed to feel sorry for me. Nevertheless, this would be a tough day of reaping consequences.

Dad insisted that I return the three dollars to each of the five customers whose orders I messed up. He gave me ten one-dollar bills, saying they were an advance on Grandma's Christmas present minus the half that went into savings. I was proficient enough in math to know I would be five dollars short, but we left the house with my box of cards anyway and no further explanation from Dad. He must have heard something from God that I hadn't.

We began by taking care of some of the problematic deliveries. Sam and Debbie chuckled at my story and said "Mr. and Mrs." was fine with them. Dad wasn't happy, but he let that one slide. Mr. and Mrs. Franks did *not* chuckle. They were not as pleased with my penmanship as Mrs. Martin was. They got their three dollars back so they could buy some plain old non-personalized cards.

I explained my mistake and attempted cover-up to the Martins. Harry had a good laugh, especially since he didn't have hair one on his head. Mrs. Martin didn't dwell on my flawed spelling since she knew this was costing me big. I gave their money back.

The "Fillups" thought the whole mix-up was a riot, considering that Mr. Phillips pumped gas at the Texaco in a nearby town. Dad even laughed at that one, but he still made me return the money.

I'd used up nine of the ten dollars, and I was worn out from explaining my slipup. Dad must have known I needed a break. He drove me around to outlying areas to deliver the correct orders. People were pleased to receive their Deluxe Correctly Personalized Christmas Greeting Cards, and I began to feel better.

Then we came to the "Cabbage" house. With only a dollar left, I didn't see how I could make this one right. Mrs. Wilson had always said God makes a way. I was providing Him with a great opportunity to prove Himself.

Dad and Mr. Cubbage talked by themselves for a minute. Then Mr. Cubbage left the room briefly. When he returned, they both walked over to me with serious expressions.

Mr. Cubbage looked over his cards while I shifted my weight back and forth from one foot to the other. Finally, he said he would take the cards along with only two dollars. He revealed that, being the church janitor, he had used white paint himself once or twice to correct a mistake. His confession would have been music to my ears if I'd had the two dollars.

I pulled a sweaty dollar bill out of my pocket and held it out to him. "This is all I have left," I mumbled to the floor. My eyes were getting misty. It had been a long day.

Mr. Cubbage took the money. "I hear the preacher has a long sermon tomorrow. I imagine there will be considerable gum chewing going on." Then he pulled a putty knife from his back pocket. "We both know where you can scrape up an honest dollar next week, don't we?"

I accepted the tool from him, relieved to return to manual labor.

Chapter 17

Vermin, Grapevines, and Gang Wars

MY ATTRACTION TO THE WOODS began when I was about five years old. Our property in Dorset contained a couple of acres of pine forest that was bisected by a small stream. I could spend hours at a time there, often returning to the house with a turtle or frog to show Mom. She took great interest in my discoveries until I showed up in the kitchen one day with a snake. Neither of us was welcome, and we barely escaped the swatter in our speedy exit.

Mom's parting words as I made my way back into the pines with the slithery serpent were emphatic: "You shouldn't play with snakes." But she didn't say I *couldn't*. So I learned early on to confine my questionable exploits to the woods.

In Tippecanoe, the kid-to-forest magnetism became even stronger. Maybe that's because my wooded playground increased thirtyfold. I romped among the trees at least once a week during the summer months. I usually went with Jerry and Kenny. Although we could enter the woods behind Jerry's house, we often followed the paved lane behind the parsonage into the trees. It passed Cookie Lady's house and ended at a huge hayfield where we could choose any of several paths to reenter the surrounding woods. We never ran out of ideas to occupy ourselves. And unless those ideas were expressly prohibited, they were worthy of our consideration.

Occasionally our excursion went no farther than the hayfield. If the farmer had mown the field recently, we might spend the day flying kites from a rise in the middle. Sometimes we attached handkerchief parachutes to the kite tails or frames with half of a square knot. With a little luck, the kite reached a decent height before the string came undone, allowing a rock weight to pull the parachute to a gentle landing.

One day, Jerry, Kenny, and I watched a parachute drift landward for the tenth time.

"This is boring," said Kenny.

Jerry and I agreed. We all sat on the ground and thought.

After a couple of minutes, Jerry said, "I've got it! Let's parachute a mouse."

"How?" I asked. "Do you expect him to stand on the rock and hold on to the string?"

"No, dummy. We can take the rock off and tie the mouse to the parachute," said Jerry. "It will be like a harness. This will be our best stunt ever."

Kenny and I were immediately in. We all left our kites and parachutes lying in the field and raced back to my house to locate a furry little paratrooper.

I often cornered mice in our garage and kept them for pets, so I knew my parents wouldn't have a problem with me handling the mouse. In fact, when I was six years old and a mouse ran across my grandparents' kitchen floor, Dad and Grandpa both yelled, "Butch, catch that mouse!" Obediently, I did. The mouse bit me, I screamed, and Dad and Grandpa both laughed. No, my parents wouldn't care about me catching the mouse. However, they might have concern for the little critter when we sent it airborne.

I didn't have any mice boarders at that time. Most of my tenants chewed out of their comfy shoebox apartments within days. Nor did we spot any lurking in the most promising mouse habitats in my garage. We managed to find one, though, in a shed in Kenny's backyard. Full of the wisdom gleaned long ago in my grandpa's kitchen, I used a pair of Dad's heavy gloves.

Back at the hayfield, we removed the rock from one parachute and replaced it with the novice parachutist. It took two of us, one wearing the gloves to hold the squirmy rodent and the other to secure the string under its front legs while trying, unsuccessfully, to avoid its teeth. It took several minutes to get our unwilling recruit hooked up. If it had known the sheer excitement it was about to experience, it surely would have been more cooperative.

We wrapped handkerchief around parachutist and tied it loosely to the kite. With great fanfare, I released the kite to the elements while Jerry controlled the string. The operation worked perfectly on the first try. At about 50 feet, the parachute came loose and quickly filled with air. As it floated earthward, the small gray creature dangled below, its front legs extended to the sides. It looked as if it was thoroughly enjoying the experience . . . or else it was in shock.

Parachute and jumper both landed safely. The three of us patted each other on our backs, celebrating our first successful training jump. Suddenly the parachute took off across the field. We took off after it. Mouse and parachute were fine, but we decided we needed to station someone near the landing spot on future drops to discourage deserters from running off with our supplies.

We were eager to try for a higher jump, so after bringing the kite down, Kenny tied the parachute-cocooned mouse on, this time with a shoelace knot. Jerry released the kite. It soared until it took all 100 yards of twine. I jerked the kite several times, but the parachute stayed secure. Funny, those shoelace knots always came loose on the playground.

We thought higher, gustier winds might do the trick so we attached more line. It wasn't long before we could barely see the kite. We had never flown one that high before.

We still had not seen the parachute drop. After ten minutes of trying to shake it loose, we reeled in the kite. To our surprise, there was no parachute or trooper. Figuring the kite must have dropped its load over the woods, we scoured the most likely area all afternoon. Our necks were sore from gazing into the trees. We finally called off our search. We could easily replace the handkerchief. As for the AWOL jumper, surely if he could chew through a shoebox, he was able to escape from a parachute harness made of string . . . I hoped.

That day marked the first and the last mouse parachute jump in the hayfield in the woods. Kenny and Jerry both suffered bites. I even got nailed through my gloves. And we had lost our first recruit. I decided it would be best if our short-lived paratrooper training remained one of my secrets of the forest.

~ ~ ~

ONE OF MY FAVORITE ACTIVITIES in the woods was playing Tarzan. We ran through the "jungle" with a troop of imaginary apes, leaped from trees, and wrestled imaginary crocodiles. And we swung on real grapevines.

Most of them were too small to support even Cheetah when he was a baby chimp, let alone Tarzan. If we were up to a challenge, there was a large boomerang vine. When we swung out, it pulled us right back into the tree. We tried to turn ourselves to come in facing the tree with our feet out so we could push off for another swing. However, more times than not, we'd just get the air knocked out of us and pick up fresh scrapes and bruises.

The only true Tarzan vine was as thick as my leg and attached as far up as I could see to an ancient hickory tree. We'd take turns grabbing the vine, climbing up on a rock ledge, and taking a running jump off into high-flying exhilaration. We sailed in a wide arc out over a deep gully and back to solid ground on the opposite side of the tree. The possibility of a 15-foot drop onto rocks below ensured that our grips remained strong.

That was never more important than on one particular swinging adventure. Jerry was sailing over the gully when, without warning, the vine sharply dropped two feet. Everyone gasped loudly. Jerry held tight and made it to safety, but we were all shaken. Though it was Jerry who got the closer look at the rocks, we all had more respect for the vine after that. From then on, we tested its security before each use by having multiple people grab it and jerk with all their might.

This seemed like another secret to best leave among the trees.

~ ~ ~

THE SUMMER AFTER SIXTH GRADE, I became interested in soldiering. Jerry, Kenny, and I would go on patrols armed with slingshots because our parents wouldn't allow us to take our Daisy air rifles to the woods unless we went solo. They suspected we would play war games—and they were probably right.

I wore Dad's old army belt equipped with canteen, machete, and ammo pouches. My pouches contained marbles or tubes of BBs, the compass and camera I had purchased with Bazooka comics, Bazooka gum, and "energy pills" to give me superhero endurance. The pills were usually penny candy, though on a healthy snack day I would pack peanuts and raisins.

We built a makeshift fort from scrap lumber scrounged from around town. It wasn't pretty, but it was ours. We hunkered down inside and peered through the gaping holes, watching for the enemy. We would be the last line of defense should an invasion befall our beloved town.

Eventually, our fort became our clubhouse. We were much too active, though, to spend much time inside. We didn't even bother to give our club a name.

While running by our headquarters one day, we skidded to a stop.

"What happened?" Kenny said as we all stared at the pile of lumber.

We knew our building skills were not the greatest, but there hadn't been a strong enough wind recently to do that kind of damage.

"Someone tore our cabin down," said Jerry in unbelief.

"Who?" Kenny asked.

"I bet it was those little kids who built that cabin on the next hill," I said.

With no discussion, we raced off with one unifying purpose—retaliation.

When we neared the rival cabin, we took up positions behind trees to watch and listen. We waited until we were sure no one was inside, then stealthily made our way to the building and took it apart board by board. Smugly, we returned to put our own clubhouse back together, though somewhat reconfigured.

Two weeks later, we found it dismantled again.

"Ah, man," said Jerry. "Not again."

"Let's just rebuild," I said.

It wasn't until we began to pull and straighten nails that we realized four boards were missing. Our only good boards.

"We don't have enough to do the whole thing," said Kenny. "We need our boards."

"This is war!" said Jerry.

"Come on guys. Let's go get our wood back," I said.

We ran all the way. Their clubhouse was a foot taller than the last time we'd torn it apart. We quickly reclaimed what was ours and turned to leave.

Then Jerry said, "Hey, let's get a couple extra."

"They aren't ours," said Kenny.

"They did it first," I said. "We're just getting back."

"Oh, yeah," Kenny agreed hesitantly.

We pried two more nice boards loose and trudged back the quarter mile, each with an armload, to rebuild once again.

Two days later, we went back to see if our clubhouse was still intact. It was. We sat inside on the dirt floor, enjoying the fact that it hadn't been vandalized again.

"Hey guys," said Kenny, "I had a dream last night that we went to jail for stealing."

"It was only two boards," said Jerry. "Besides they stole more than that from us."

"And they tore down our clubhouse first," I added.

A couple of long minutes passed in the cramped space as the consequences of our deed sank in.

"I don't want to go to jail," Kenny whimpered.

"Okay. I've got an idea," said Jerry. "Let's take their boards back and nail them back up."

"And let's throw in an extra board, one of our good ones," I added. "They can't arrest us for giving something away."

We completed our penance. After that, we never minded if we found our clubhouse dismantled. We had way more fun building it than we did sitting around inside it. And the incident helped me realize that I much preferred rambling through my woods than rumbling in them.

~ ~ ~

IT WAS NO WONDER I spent so much of my boyhood in the woods. They provided abundant freedom for me to run and explore and offered endless opportunities for my imagination to soar like the high-flying kite. While I was only aware of having a fantastic time, lessons were drifting into my life: having compassion for defenseless creatures, taking responsibility for being a safer daredevil, and respecting the rights of rivals. The should nots were being replaced with want tos. Some things were better *not* left in the woods of Tippecanoe.

Chapter 18

The Goat Woman

IT WAS ELEVEN O'CLOCK and blacker than pitch. I shuddered under my blanket with my eyes wide open, the kind of wide open that attempts to sharpen your hearing. Someone was on the other side of the canvas wall. I was sure everyone in the tent could hear my heart pounding. Worse than that, so could *she*.

The day had begun with no indication of it being anything other than a normal August day. Late in the afternoon, my whole family walked up the steep alley behind the church to eat supper with the Fraziers. As soon as the meal was over, Dad bugged out for home. Mom and Paula stayed to help Mrs. Frazier with the Tupperware party she was throwing that evening. Dave also stayed behind. His job would be to entertain the ladies with his cuteness. Mr. Frazier retreated to his basement workshop. Lloyd, the Frazier boys, and I would enjoy a night of camping out in the backyard. Or so we thought.

Just after six o'clock, our band of five adventurers took off for the woods where we would play in the hills before darkness corralled us in our tent for the night. Though we had just eaten a huge meal—and were burping like Earl Silas Tupper's bowls—we detoured to the Cookie Lady's house to see if she had any treats stashed away. Sure enough, Miss Trulah rounded up some huge oatmeal chocolate chip cookies and served them with a smile.

"What are you boys doing up here this time of day?"

"We're going to swing on the grapevine and then camp out in my yard all night," said Carl. "Maybe we'll see the Goat Woman in the woods."

"She's really, really ugly," said Tony.

"She's the meanest woman in the world," Jerry added.

"I'm not scared of her," I said, convincing no one—not even me.

"Why do you say such things about her? Has she ever hurt anyone?" Miss Trulah's smile had vanished. I had never seen her so serious. It sounded as though she was hurt, but I couldn't figure out why.

"She does terrible things to kids," said Lloyd.

"Like what?"

"We don't know exactly cuz she drags her victims down to her cave on the lake." Though Lloyd was only eight, he was well-versed on Goat Woman lore.

"Well boys, don't be too quick to judge people, even so-called monsters, without knowing all the facts."

Eager to bring back Miss Trulah's smile, we all agreed to curb our judgment. We said goodbye and raced away with a second round of cookies, our attention already shifted to outracing each other to the grapevine. However, before we were even out of earshot, Carl had forgotten our agreement and yelled for all the woods to hear, "I dare you, wretched Goat Woman, to come and get us!"

Carl wouldn't be afraid of an entire herd of goat people. I wanted to look just as bold in front of my brother, so I hollered an insult to the hoofed creature as loudly as I dared. My loud came out only slightly above a whisper, though, because I was sure that if she heard me I'd be dead.

The first stories about the goat woman had surfaced a year before. Some older boys swore they saw her on this very hill, and they made sure all the kids heard about her. Since then, spottings had occurred throughout the woods east of SR 8. Many of them were around Clendening Lake, but no one had yet found the location of her cave. I desperately hoped she was following the rules we had created for her. Rule number one was that she never left her cave until dark. That would give us a good hour of fearless play before we needed to start home.

When the sun began fading behind the hill, five nowhere-near-worn-out adventurers reluctantly headed to the safety of the backyard where Mr. Frazier had pitched a tent for us near the edge of the woods. We started a fire and waited for a good blaze to develop. In the meantime, we played an energetic game of tag using the marshmallow sticks. The twilight provided sufficient visibility to protect our eyes from misplaced tags. Eventually we settled down to roast marshmallows and play with the fire.

Around ten o'clock, the only illumination came from the dying embers and a glow through the kitchen window. My family had gone home, but Mrs. Frazier must have been cleaning up from the party. We had devoured all the marshmallows and didn't feel like any more fun and games. We crawled into the tent and staked out our territories. We talked for a while, but before long Carl was snoring. Then Tony dropped off. Next, Lloyd's sleepy voice disappeared from the conversation. I was almost out myself when I heard something brush against the tent.

"Jerry, did you hear that?" I whispered loudly.

"Yeah," he whispered back.

"What was it?" I asked.

"I dunno. Maybe some leaves blowing against the tent?"

"Maybe." My voice was barely audible. I was not at all convinced.

We lay frozen in silence . . . listening. A minute later, we heard the sound again.

"That's not leaves," I said. "It's something big. It's rubbing against the tent on purpose."

"Butch, you don't think it's the *Goat* Woman, do you?"

"Yeah, I do."

"But rule number two. She's not supposed to go in backyards." Jerry's voice grew louder with each word.

"I guess no one told her the rules," I said. "We'd better wake up the guys."

Tony and Lloyd were wide awake as soon as we told them Goat Woman was outside the tent. However, nothing could awaken Carl when the sandman got hold of him. It irritated me that he could sleep through this. He and his big mouth were the reason Goat Woman was standing three feet from our quaking bodies to begin with.

We all agreed to run for the house. I peered through a slit in the tent door to make sure the way was clear. I couldn't see a thing; Mr. and Mrs. Frazier must have forgotten to flip the back porch light on for us. At the risk of revealing ourselves to our adversary, I turned my flashlight on. We needed the light to guarantee we were heading straight for the door. Every second would count.

No one wanted to go first. Then we heard the *meh-eh-eh meh-eh-eh* outside and jumped up as one, falling over each other as we wrapped ourselves in whatever blankets we could grab. We tore out of the tent, nearly knocking it over, and left a snoring Carl as a sacrifice to Goat Woman.

We tripped and screamed the whole way to the house. Relieved to be safely inside, we collapsed on the living room floor and stared at the ceiling as the adrenaline subsided. Within a half hour, we had all dropped off to sleep.

I awoke the next morning to Carl coming in for breakfast. I about jumped out of my skin when I saw he was still with us. He, on the other hand, seemed oblivious to his brush with death. Mr. and Mrs. Frazier said nothing about finding the four of us sleeping inside. They probably just thought we'd gotten spooked by sounds in the night—and they would have been more right than they could have imagined.

When we packed up our gear, my flashlight was missing. Lloyd and I looked all over the yard. We couldn't find it and I finally gave up, happy that was *all* I'd lost on this campout.

I needed to get over this Goat Woman thing. I was 12 now and in less than two weeks, I would occupy a seat in the seventh-grade class. I had some fast growing up to do. But not just about childish fears. I had been noticing the eighth-grade boys I'd be sharing a room and a teacher with. Some stood a head taller than me, and they were already shaving.

~ ~ ~

A FEW DAYS AFTER the harrowing encounter with the Goat Woman, my family spent an afternoon in the country visiting the Wilsons. Fred and Sharon lived three miles east of town. Sharon Wilson, sister-in-law to my youth leader, was the seventh- and eighth-grade teacher. Their son Randy was home from college for the summer.

Paula, Lloyd, and I loved going to the Wilson farm. There were fun things to do that we didn't have in our small parsonage lot. Across the road was the best creek ever. In the woods by our house, we had gullies that had water only during a good rain; the Wilson's creek always flowed, eventually emptying into Clendening Lake. We waded barefoot; we threw stones into the water to splash each other; we turned rocks over searching for crawdads; and we caught gobs of tadpoles, frogs, and salamanders.

Behind their farmhouse was forest that encircled several hay-fields, all of which followed the steep contours of the hills. The wooded areas themselves were not so different from our own, but it was new territory to explore on the opposite side of the lake from where we lived.

They also had a barn. A thick rope hung in the middle from a beam high above the dirt floor. At one end of the barn, bales of hay were piled high. An eight-foot mound of loose hay stood at the opposite end. We swung on the rope from the bales and dropped into the scratchy haystack. When we tired of that, we burrowed into the mound and popped out to scare each other. We never ran out of things to do at the Wilson's.

After we splashed and swung for several hours on that sum-mer afternoon, Randy came out to the barn and gassed up the tractor. Randy was as cool as his cousin Tim, only instead of a hot rod he gave us rides on his orange Allis-Chalmers. Lloyd and I hopped onto the heavy bar in back and clung to the seat as we chugged off to the various hayfields, checking for hay that was ready to bale.

It was difficult to talk over the roar of the engine, but I just had to tell Randy about the Goat Woman episode. I thought he should know since the Wilson farm extended to the lake. Her cave could even be on his property.

"So you actually saw this Goat Woman?" Randy asked.

"No, we didn't see her. It was blacker than coal that night. But we heard her. She scraped against the tent."

"Did she say anything?" he asked.

"Nothing we could understand," I said.

"She was talkin' goat language," Lloyd yelled.

Randy finished his rounds and dropped us off at the house. "Thanks for warning me about the Goat Woman," he said. "I'll sure keep my eyes peeled for her."

"Let me know if you find her cave," I said.

"Will do, Goat Boy," he said as he drove back to the barn.

I sure hoped *that* name wouldn't stick. Who wants to be known as the son of Goat Woman?

~ ~ ~

SCHOOL WOULD START IN A WEEK. I was sitting around the house waiting for the next exciting idea to hit when Dad asked me if I'd like to fish a couple of hours at the lake. Pow! That was it. Five minutes later, my gear was in the car.

It was a warm, almost stifling, day. A lazy day. The perfect kind of day to sit on the bank, throw a line in the water, and wait for a fish to wander by for a game of hide-and-seek with the bobber.

After we settled in, Dad said, "How are you feeling about school starting?"

"OK. I'll miss Mrs. Martin, but at least I know Mrs. Wilson. She's nice."

"Yes, she is," Dad agreed.

After a bit, I said, "The eighth-grade boys are awful big."

"Yes, they are. That bother you?" Dad asked.

I shrugged. "A little."

"Well, don't rush things. Next year *you'll* be a big eighth grader."

I hadn't thought that far ahead. It made me feel just a tad better about the upcoming school year. But a few whiskers starting up on my chin would have made me feel even better.

We continued to watch our bobbers. It didn't look as though the fish were in the mood to play.

"How was the campout at Jerry's?" Dad asked.

"Great!" I tried to sound upbeat.

"I heard you slept inside the house." Nothing seemed to get by my parents. "Get scared?" he asked.

"We heard scratching and mehing."

"Mighta been a bobcat."

"Really?"

"Few around here."

More silence while I thought about that one. A bobcat was almost as bad as a goat monster.

"This yours?" Dad said as he pulled a flashlight out of his pocket.

"Wow. Thanks!"

"Your friend asked me to give it back."

"Carl?"

"Nope. Miss Trulah."

The gears in my brain were working much faster than they should have been on such a slow, lazy day. I was trying to figure out how Miss Trulah got my flashlight. We saw her long before I used it at the tent.

"You boys saw her that night?"

"Yeah," I said slowly. "We stopped by for cookies."

"Well, you boys hurt her feelings."

"How?" I asked. "We never did anything to her. Honest!"

"You made fun of Goat Woman."

"But we didn't say anything about *her*." I was ready to defend myself on this point.

"The Goat Woman is her sister."

Now it was just getting too weird. I stared at Dad with my mouth gaping open.

He continued. "Miss Trulah told me how she figures the whole story got started. Last fall her sister Genevieve was enjoying an evening walk in the woods. She had curlers in her hair and must have been a sight. Two older boys came down the same path. After they passed her, she heard them laughing and saying something about an old goat."

I waited, still in shock.

"When did that Goat Woman story start going around school?" Dad asked.

"'Bout a year ago, I guess."

"Well, those boys are probably the ones who started it. Any idea how Miss Trulah got wind of it?"

"We mentioned Goat Woman to her a few times," I said. "But we never knew about her sister. I never wanted to hurt Miss Trulah."

"The other night, she thought she'd play a little trick on you guys."

"That was *her* outside our tent? No way."

"Yes, it was her," said Dad. "I guess she got you good."

"Yes, she did," I said. A chuckle soon gave way to a belly laugh when I pictured Miss Trulah standing outside our tent imitating a goat. Dad joined in. It took a full minute to laugh ourselves out.

Then Dad got serious again. "Just because guys are older and bigger than you doesn't mean they always act grownup. You'll do fine in Mrs. Wilson's class. Your size isn't everything."

I felt a little bigger after that fishing trip. Not in stature, but I would have a tall secret going with me into seventh grade: Jerry and I would know the truth about the Goat Woman.

~ ~ ~

SEVENTH GRADE turned out to be great. Mrs. Wilson was a fantastic teacher, which helped me to not miss Mrs. Martin so much. We did cool projects and went on field trips. Sometimes we took nature hikes back behind the school.

On one of those walks, we gathered samples for our leaf collections. Jerry and I hung back near the end of the line so we wouldn't get trampled every time we stopped for a specimen. Two of the towering—and most annoying—eighth graders were a few students ahead of us, whispering and giggling. Every few steps, they turned around to look at us.

With Mrs. Wilson occupied at the head of the line answering questions, Darryl and Mike stopped to let students pass them. When we reached them, they started in on us.

"Why are you boys way back here?" asked Mike. "Don't you

know Goat Woman picks off stragglers and carries them off to her cave?"

"Yeah, their families never see them again," said Darryl. He motioned toward the middle of the line. "You'd better run up there and hide among the girls."

"Get lost," Jerry told them. "We're not afraid of you. And we're not afraid of Goat Woman."

"Hey, Goat Woman!" Mike yelled. "Come and get these munchkins. They're bite size."

"You don't scare us," I said. "You don't know what you're talking about. *We* know who Goat Woman is."

"Yeah," Jerry added.

Just then, Mrs. Wilson's voice reverberated through the woods. "Class, stop." Her teacher-sense told her something was going on that had nothing to do with foliage. The students parted as she barreled down the trail and stopped a foot from the four of us.

She had to look up to speak to Darryl and Mike. "What are you boys yelling about?"

While they searched for an answer, Jerry said, "They're trying to scare us by calling Goat Woman to come and eat us."

"Such nonsense," she said. "You are both almost 14. Certainly too old to believe in monsters. You need to start acting like young men."

"We don't believe in the Goat Woman, Mrs. Wilson," I said. Beside me, Jerry was shaking his head in agreement.

"Good for you, boys," she said. Then she added, "You've got some nice leaves there."

Looking back to Darryl and Mike, she asked, "Where are *your* leaves?"

"We haven't found any good ones yet," said Darryl.

"I suggest you find some soon. If you don't come back with a sizable assortment, I will double your assignment. Understand?"

"Yes ma'am," said Mike.

"Yes ma'am," Darryl parroted.

"You two come with me. Maybe you'll have better luck in the front of the line." As Mrs. Wilson led them off, they turned and made ugly faces at us. Apparently, they weren't ready to be young men yet.

Jerry and I maintained our serious demeanors until Mrs. Wilson reached her forward post. My friend grinned at me as he took a bite from an imaginary cookie. I knew what he was saying. Like him, I couldn't wait till we were able to get to Miss Trulah's house after school and tell her how we had served up justice that day.

We didn't hear Goat Woman mentioned as much after that nature walk. Unless you count those occasions when Jerry and I relived the experience with Miss Trulah over cookies and milk—with the complete approval of the resident gargoyles.

Chapter 19

Flying with No Parachute
and Boating in a Tippy "Canoe"

WHEN ENGINEERS BUILT SR 8 through Tippecanoe, they had to
remove the side of one of the town's highest hills, exposing solid
rock. I sit on a terraced drop-off created from the cutting and
gaze over the landscape far below. I pick out the houses of my
friends, stores I frequent, and landmarks that are my life here.
Stillwater Creek cuts a satiny ribbon through fields rich in corn
and hay.

I take special note of a large clearing across the road where I
plan to end today's excursion. Beside me rests a grand wooden
glider, ready for its maiden flight over the town. I don a helmet
(a hardhat from Dad's sawmill days) and climb into the cockpit.
It lacks restraints, but the snug fit should prevent me from falling out.

A gust of wind launches the craft, and a strong thermal lifts it
up toward the clouds. My excitement surpasses anything I've
ever experienced on the ground. This must be what an eagle feels

as he soars effortlessly above the trees. The plane's agility and responsiveness to the controls amaze me. I make a hard left turn and begin a sweeping circle of my small town.

As I drift over the school, I see all my classmates and teachers gathered on the playground, waving skyward. The clamor of their exclamations reaches me: "Way to go Butch!" "How cool!" "Can I have a ride?" "I don't hate you, Butch." I'm relieved that no one is wielding a slingshot. I wonder how I got out of class today. Oh well. I tip my wings in a salute. Carl will probably start construction on his own glider after school, and I make a mental note to cancel any flights when he is airborne.

Ahead, I spot a wisp of smoke. It's Henry waving a lit cattail torch as though he's knighting me with a sword for valiantly conquering the skies. Across the road, Mrs. Wilson looks up from pruning her rosebushes. Her beaming smile is so large I can see it from way up here. Her son Tim sits in his '41 Ford convertible, looking as if he would trade rides in an instant. He gives me a hearty thumbs-up.

Dad and Mom watch from the front yard of the parsonage to celebrate my big moment, praying that the altitude doesn't bring on a fainting spell. Mr. Cubbage is next door, freshening up the white paint on the church sign. He raises his brush when he sees me. I bet he's wondering how many boxes of greeting cards I had to sell to get *this* plane.

On the hill to my left, I see Miss Trulah gathering eggs for a fresh batch of cookies. Too bad I can't land this craft in her yard and pick up a peanut butter snack to go.

East of her house lie the woods I have explored endlessly. Where the trees stop, the sparkling blue water of Lake Clendening appears. If it were the ocean, it couldn't occupy a more significant place in my heart. I proceed over the dam, near the best picnic spot in the world.

Next I circle over Dr. Trimnell's home. He's outside, holding something in each hand. I drop a few feet until I can make out what it is. He is ready with two of his longest needles in case I come in for too rough of a landing. That is great motivation for me to stay focused.

I bank right and cross over SR 8. Two boys I don't know are sitting on Johnny Appleseed's porch getting a whittling lesson. Johnny takes a moment to acknowledge the fine workmanship flying overhead.

I begin my descent, passing over Stillwater Creek, close enough to see the giant carp just under the surface. Hey, there's a corroded steel tub up on the bank. *That* sure stirs up a memory. But right now I have to concentrate on bringing this bird in.

Even though I've never had a flying lesson, I know instinctively how to deploy the spoilers to reduce the lift and increase the drag. I deftly control the glide path and bring my machine down to my chosen spot in the clearing.

After my exhilarating flight and safe landing . . . I wake up. I lie in bed savoring the encouragement and support I have just experienced from those who knew me best. I wasn't 11 anymore though. I was 31 years old and still dreaming about my Tipp years.

Now I am more than twice that age. Although I no longer have dreams of gliders or Tippecanoe, the images of my small-town life are still pleasantly etched in my memory.

~ ~ ~

SOON AFTER MY FAMILY MOVED to Tippecanoe, my Uncle Jim took me for a canoe ride on Lake Clendening. I began right then dreaming of having my own canoe to paddle down Stillwater Creek.

I loved fishing in that creek. Once I pulled out a catfish with legs! I ran home with it, knowing I would soon be talking to the *Freeport Press* reporter again. And this time, it was an honest catch with a pole and line. Then Mr. Wilson, my youth leader's husband, informed me that my "catfish" was not a new or mutant species. It was just a common mudpuppy.

Still, I was certain that some undiscovered creature must inhabit those waters. I needed my canoe so I could begin my Stillwater Creek expeditions. My friends and I had built rafts in the past from logs we found along the edge of the creek. We tied them together with rope, but they always came loose. Remembering this, I thought constructing a canoe might be beyond my capabilities just now.

One day I found a large, round galvanized steel tub on the bank. It was four feet wide and two feet deep. There was a little rust but I couldn't find any holes. And it was solid. It sure didn't look like a canoe, but it was worth a try.

It was nearly impossible to keep my new craft upright. By accident, I discovered I could control it better with several inches of water in the bottom. One time I floated about the length of a football field before it tipped, all the while slowly spinning and taking in a 360-degree view of the stream and its banks. Fortunately I had witnesses, not only to vouch for my partially successful journey but also to throw me a rope when I capsized.

~ ~ ~

ALTHOUGH I SPENT only three years of my young life in Tippecanoe, my experiences during that time would fill a treasure chest. But I didn't store them away; rather I cashed those golden nuggets in long ago to purchase who I am today.

They bought me the feeling of being valued. The adults in my town had no small hand in that. They watched over me as if I were their own, each one teaching me priceless lessons. I think of Henry, Trulah Gilbody, and Johnny Appleseed. My soul would be poorer today if I had been shielded from these "quirky" grown-ups.

They bought me knowledge and, more importantly, ways to apply it. Much of what I learned about the three R's, the Bible, and life in general took place during my Tipp years. And sometimes I learned those lessons simultaneously in the classroom. After all, where better to apply life lessons than where so much life happens.

They bought me direction in life. Adults were not reluctant to tell this little squirt that some things are right and some things are wrong. But yet, I was permitted to test many of those things myself—while not being safeguarded from the consequences of my mistakes. They let me learn the hard way.

And finally, they bought me the freedom to explore, both places and ideas. My feet and bike took me all over town and the surrounding landscapes. My mind was free to be creative—sometimes dangerously so. It was a world of sharp knives, exploding carbide, smoking pant legs, sled pileups, and perilous grapevines. When I think back to being a kid—one that my fellow fast-food boomers would appreciate—I always find myself in Tippecanoe.

I can't put a price tag on these possessions. Though they came into my life over half a century ago, they still guide my steps and help make me *me*.

Being a kid in my small town was like flying in my dream-glider without restraints or a parachute. Ahead was adventure, excitement, the unknown—along with the possibility of turbulent winds or a bumpy landing. But I always felt secure, nestled into the cockpit of my family and neighbors. I don't remember ever feeling unsafe during those years.

My tippy "canoe" ride in the Stillwater and life in my small town may have both been a little unsteady sometimes, but on both counts, a little tipping never hurt me one bit.

Epilogue

50 Years Later

IT'S A WARM, SUNNY SATURDAY in August 2015 as Bonnie and I near our destination. We traveled 220 miles this morning to take part in the First "Dam" Tippecanoe Two-Mile Walk. I picked up a flyer about the event when I passed through earlier this summer. The walk is in conjunction with the annual Tippecanoe Volunteer Fire Department Homecoming Festival. The community has organized multiple activities throughout the day. More is on my mind, though, than just the scheduled events. One particular thought elbows its way to the forefront: Will I find anything to connect with those middle school years over half a century ago?

The shady country road curves in a quarter-mile semi-circle and ends in a parking lot. On our right is Clendening Dam where Dad and I used to fish. To the left is Clendening Lake Dam Park, the site of Labor Day picnics and Easter sunrise services. I've returned to the town that holds my fondest childhood memories. Excitement stirs in me.

I drive past the gathering of walkers and park at the far end of the lot. Bonnie and I cross the rectangular lawn, snuggled into the forest that surrounds the lake, and join over 50 others, none of whom we know. The participants range from a 70ish-year-old woman to a baby in a stroller. Everyone appears to know each other, and they chat in small groups about their families and recent activities. We look for some friendly faces to begin getting acquainted.

Our first stop is at a millstone turned on its side and covered with bright yellow event T-shirts. We pick ours up, pull them on over our other shirts, and begin a conversation with two sisters. They are considerably younger than I am, but they have heard of Dad. Their mother had attended one of his churches and had shared amusing pastor stories with them. It hasn't taken long to make my first connection.

The next friendly face belongs to a man my son's age. Does he also know someone from my past? Three sentences into our conversation, I discover he is Hank's son. That would be the Hank I had a scuffle with in fifth grade. Our mutual association astonishes us. The young man says his father might be at the firehouse later for lunch. I look forward to seeing Hank. I want to make sure there are no lingering hostilities between us.

It is time for the walk to begin. The organizer gathers everyone to give us instructions. She follows with a prayer, not only for our safety but also that as we walk, we will breathe in the Holy Spirit as well as oxygen. Wow! Just like Mrs. Martin starting out her classes with prayer. I appreciate the words spoken here, and that folks in Tippecanoe still look to a power greater than themselves in their everyday lives.

We begin in the middle of the pack and follow a shifting yellow form of shirts out of the park. We walk the same route we drove earlier. The shade gives way to a brilliant sun. I can't tell if it is shining brighter in my eyes or deep in my soul. I'm back on my turf where I used to fly along these roads on my bike as free as the surrounding air. We reach the marked turnaround and complete our two miles back to the park. I barely notice being tired and hot from the exercise; I'm too eager to see what yet awaits me today.

We join others at the Methodist Church for the pancake breakfast. How many hours did I sit in this basement attending Sunday school or practicing the piano? I could supply music to go with our meal today, but I don't see the piano. That's probably just as well; I've grown a little rusty.

The serving line is short. Cheerful church ladies serve our food on what looks to be the same plates used here in the '60s, a blue willow pattern. If so, this is some durable dishware. After they fill my blue willow mug with coffee, Bonnie and I find a spot at a table covered with plastic blue gingham.

The man sitting across from us looks familiar. Before I can pull up a name, he greets me. "Hey, Butch." Immediately, I recognize him as Randy Wilson, the son of my seventh-grade teacher. We reminisce about the tractor rides he gave me and my exploration of the hills between his house and Lake Clendening.

I meet the mother of the two sisters at the park. She does indeed remember my dad, though she must have been quite young when he pastored here. We exchange stories of his mischievous antics.

I see Mrs. Martin's son. Though he is several years my senior, I knew him well. We heartily shake hands and catch up on the main happenings of the past several decades. He takes us upstairs to see the sanctuary. I notice few changes since I warmed the pews over 50 years ago. Mrs. Martin's personal organ sits to the side of the altar; her family donated it to the church after her passing. The front row of seats sits farther from the pulpit, a safer distance from the long arm of the preacher. I don't think to check under the pews to see how much gum my successors have plastered there since Gumboy retired.

We leave the church and begin a walking tour of the town. I want to share my favorite spots with Bonnie. We amble along the alley behind the parsonage and reach Henry's yard. My heart misses a beat; the house is gone. Grass has grown in so I can't tell a structure ever stood here. Henry's hill seems smaller than I remember. It needs a king-sized blanket of snow to create the grandness that lives in my mind. I wonder if this hill still challenges the town youth.

We retrace our steps to the church, turn up the lane, and take the trail above the alley. A sweetness drifts through the trees, but the aroma bypasses my senses and lodges in my mind where it keeps company with the sledding hill. The Cookie Lady's house is not here, either. Pieces of rusted trucks and a bit of stone foundation decorate the area. Vegetation grows over everything. My taste buds, and heart, must settle for bittersweetness.

I hope at least Johnny's cabin still stands. We walk to the other side of town to his property. Zero for three on the houses. Through the green sea of wild growth, many years in the making, we spot a corroded pipe protruding from a stone wall. Perhaps it is the conduit that carried Johnny's delicious spring water. I begin to understand how long a half-century is.

Something else becomes clearer to me as well. I can feel the presence of those fine adults who helped shape my character. Though their physical dwellings are no longer here, their spirits live on in my heart. This eases my sadness at encountering such drastic changes to my childhood town.

We head back toward the church. Many houses are showing the effects of time. As far as I can tell, Tippecanoe has added few new dwellings since I lived here. We return to the car and drive to my old school, which became the new home of the Washington Township Fire Department in 2000. It looks the same except for the four firehouse doors that have replaced the side of the building where Mrs. Martin's and Mrs. Wilson's classrooms were.

Many festival goers are gathered at the firehouse: listening to the entertainment outside the building; enjoying barbecue pork, barbecue chicken, and fish in the cafeteria; reminiscing over the photographs depicting local history, which line the hallway. Inside, I see an upperclassman two years ahead of me. She remembers me. She shows us around the building.

Mrs. Martin's old room is at the end of the short hall and on the left. It is now absent of chalkboards and desks. One end wall houses various supplies and equipment, some in raised storage compartments and the rest occupying floor space. The opposite wall is empty except for a few fire extinguishers huddled in the corner of the room. Along the side wall is a rack of 40 or so rolled up fire hoses. Two more hoses hang on a rack on wheels that divides the room into two bays for emergency vehicles. What a fun classroom this would make. The two huge doors are open. They would have been handy at dismissal time when I was a student.

We walk back down the hall toward the cafeteria. Our tour guide says Michelle is working in the kitchen. She disappears and quickly returns with Michelle, who no longer has pigtails. She doesn't remember the scissors incident. I am relieved to learn that I didn't cut her hair in sixth grade. Until now, I wasn't sure if I did or not.

Michelle returns to the kitchen. Bonnie and I check out the food. We are in line getting barbecue chicken when I run into Hank. I have a pleasant, conflict-free conversation with him. That fight in Mrs. Martin's class must have settled everything. Hank doesn't even remember it.

We see Henry's granddaughter at one of the tables. She was one year ahead of me, in Sarah's class, and she lived with Henry. Sometimes she joined the sledding gang in her yard. We sit down to eat with her. She recalls the girls teasing my brother by calling him Peaches.

We finish eating and wander outside. A large shelter stands in the center of our old airfield, what used to be the playground. Mom's friend Marge sits at one of the picnic tables talking with a lady I don't know. Marge is more surprised to see Butch than I am to find her here. We exchange family news and ancient memories.

I spotted Tim Wilson earlier in a group of men in the shelter. He is alone now, so I approach him. Astonishment registers in his eyes when he sees my face from the past. I ask if he still sings. He does. In fact, we just missed hearing him. While we ate, he sang on a small stage set up in the yard for the day. We talk of the hot rod I remember, which was several cars ago.

The parade of floats and fire department vehicles is yet to come, and more entertainment will follow it into the evening, but we need to start home. We have several hours to drive.

I came today with no expectations of seeing anyone I knew, but it has been a mini school reunion. I am sorry not to see the guys I hung out with though. It would be great to relive our adventures. Sarah isn't here, either. I am left to wonder if she still doesn't hate me.

I say goodbye to Tippecanoe again and drive away content. This day is better than I ever imagined it would be. It is great reconnecting with friends and reliving pieces of my childhood. For a few hours, I once again experience the close-knit community I grew up in. I discover small-town Ohio still exists. And it still feels safe and secure.

ACKNOWLEDGMENTS

Many people offered valuable feedback on my manuscript. We greatly appreciate the gifts of their time and talents.

Thanks to my beta readers: George Castleberry, Susan Michaels, Brenda Murphy, Karen Power, and Joan Young. They made it through the entire book and were still awake enough to share their thoughtful observances with us.

Thanks to all the other generous souls who read parts of the book and shared their questions, insights, and encouragement: Dave Baker, Joan Berkemeyer, Dolores Birkle, Russell and Anne Gastright, Brenda Hall, Becky Hancock, Peggy Hoffman, Rick Iles, Jim Korpik, Mark Marchok, Chris McIntyre, Richard Morgan, Steve and Jane Onspaugh, Susan Parker, Jon Perry, John and Darleen Rethman, Randall Roberts, Bob Schaffner, Jeanne Schneider, Matt and Jayne Spencer, Dewayne Thomas, and Tom Williams.

Phyllis Dickey, Bob McConnell, and Jerry Green answered my questions about Tippecanoe in the early '60s. I made very few inquiries, however, so don't blame them for the contents of this memoir.

Kudos to Bonnie for not only editing this book but for her considerable co-writing as well. There's nothing like working on a big project with my sweetheart and my best friend.

Many thanks to the real Trulah Gilbody who has no connection whatsoever to the Cookie Lady. I simply loved her name and she graciously allowed me to borrow it for a character of my choosing in the book.

And thanks to God for helping me to recall events that occurred almost 60 years ago. Please don't hold Him responsible for the parts I might have made up.

Book Discussion Questions

The Book

1. What do you think CW Spencer's purpose was in writing *Safe and Secure in a Tippy Canoe*? Was he making a cultural statement or just reliving a happy childhood? Or did his purpose fall somewhere in between?

2. Discuss CW's writing style. Was it easy for you as the reader to connect with him?

3. Were there any gaps in Butch's life in Tippecanoe that you wish the author had filled in? Were there places you thought he shared more than necessary?

4. Did the book cover draw you into the story? Did it accurately represent what you read?

5. The book looks back nearly 60 years. Do you think it has lasting interest or value that would cause people to still be reading it in 60 more years? Explain.

The Story

6. Can you identify with any aspects or activities of Butch's childhood? If so, which ones?

7. What phrases, passages, or stories stand out to you as memorable? Do you have a favorite incident from the book?

8. How does CW portray his life growing up in Tippecanoe? What would you like and dislike most about growing up as a child in a small town like his?

9. CW describes his childhood town as being a close-knit community. Everyone knew each other. All the women were mothers to him. Do you consider your community to be close-knit? If so, in what ways? If not, what are some things you can do to help create this type of community around you?

10. In what ways did Mrs. Martin, Butch's fifth- and sixth-grade teacher, have a lasting positive influence on him? What teacher had a similar role in your life, and in what specific ways did he or she affect you?

11. In Tippecanoe, the scary story of the Goat Woman circulated among the children. Growing up, did you hear any local lore, whether frightening or humorous? Did you believe it? Do you think it was based on any truth?

12. Following Butch's laughing fit in church, he expected his father to "unleash his wrath on me in front of his flock." Instead his father bestowed grace on him. What was Butch's response? Tell about a time you had grace extended to you and the affect it had on you.

13. CW returned to his childhood town of Tippecanoe 50 years after his family moved away. What changes did he find? In what ways had it remained the same? What emotions did he experience?

14. Have you gone back to a treasured childhood place after many years have passed? How was it different? What was your reaction?

Social Issues

15. According to the events CW shared in his memoir, do you feel he lacked necessary supervision during his years in Tippecanoe? Explain.

16. Did this book cause you to question any facets of how you raised or plan to raise your children?

17. What changes in the world since the 1960s do you think have had the greatest impact on how parents raise their children today?

18. The free-range parenting movement advocates raising safe and independent children without being overprotective. Do you think in today's world that a balance can be reached between safety restrictions and freedom in raising children? Why or why not?

19. Since the years CW spent in Tippecanoe, many safety laws have been passed, such as mandatory seat belts. New health warnings seem to be announced every week: trans fats increase the risk of heart disease, secondhand smoke causes cancer, hot coffee will burn you. What, if any, safety measures do you think should be legislated, or do you think they should all be left to the discretion of the individual? Are health warnings out of control, or do you welcome the knowledge?

20. In 1960, Butch's classroom had a Bible verse displayed on the wall and Mrs. Martin began the school year with a prayer. In 1980, the U.S. Supreme Court ruled that a Kentucky statute requiring the Ten Commandments to be posted in public classrooms was unconstitutional because, they said, it lacked a non-religious purpose. In your opinion, do such displays do harm or good to children?

Also by CW Spencer

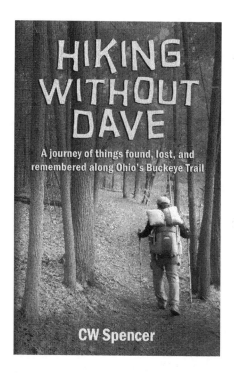

Following the suicide of his brother, CW Spencer found himself in a pit of despair and guilt. His search for healing began with one step and continued over 1,400 miles of the Buckeye Trail in Ohio as he found renewed meaning for his life. In *Hiking Without Dave*, he shares his adventures on the trail as well as moving and often humorous memories of his brother Dave. Discover for yourself the hope that can be found by taking that first step.

Available at Amazon.com

About the Author

CW Spencer grew up in northeastern Ohio. After graduating from Asbury University in Wilmore, Kentucky, he taught middle school science in northern Kentucky for 27 years. While teaching, he met his future wife Bonnie. They have been married 30 years and reside in Fort Thomas, Kentucky. CW began hiking and writing after retiring. He is the author of *Hiking Without Dave*. He also enjoys volunteer work and tootling around in his classic truck.

Visit CW's website: http://cwspencer.com/

Contact CW: cw@cwspencer.com

54013120R00093

Made in the USA
Columbia, SC
24 March 2019